I0605475

In this thoroughly researched and wonderfully written gem of a book, Grace Hamman recovers wisdom from a time before modernity's assault on the garden of the soul. In *Ask of Old Paths,* we really do find "something a little wild and beautiful." I love this book!

Brian Zahnd, author of
The Wood Between the Worlds

Ask of Old Paths retrieves more than the language of virtue and vice—it turns to Christian history to recover a robust theology of a whole and holy human life. Grace Hamman offers us a rare treasure—rich theology and history presented in an engaging and accessible manner for the sake of actual human lives. This is a book that will not only teach you about the virtues and vices but also inspire you to deeper thought and greater faithfulness.

Kaitlyn Schiess, author of
The Ballot and the Bible and cohost of the *Holy Post*

In *Ask of Old Paths,* Grace Hamman offers readers a bountiful gift, retrieving ancient wisdom for modern-day believers and seekers. Equipped with the insights of a scholar and the humility of a fellow pilgrim, Hamman guides readers on the path of virtue toward a flourishing life in and with Christ. Readers willing to take this journey will be challenged, relieved, and ultimately transformed.

Rev. Claude Atcho, pastor of
Church of the Resurrection (Charlottesville, VA)
and author of *Rhythms of Faith*
and *Reading Black Books*

With obvious delight and exquisite clarity, Grace Hamman guides us through the medieval garden of the soul, identifying both the strangling weeds of the seven capital vices and the fragrant, lush virtues we can cultivate as remedies. Under her tutelage, medieval Christianity becomes a rich resource instead of an intimidating pile of dusty manuscripts or bizarre images. Hamman gently reintroduces us to the language of virtues, helping us recognize the wisdom that remains present in words and ideas that may seem old-fashioned or even oppressive. The book is an invitation to wholeness, walking old paths to meet the challenges of our present lives.

Dr. Elissa Yukiko Weichbrodt, author of *Redeeming Vision* and professor at Covenant College

A wise and beautiful work of scholarship and devotion. Grace Hamman brings her immense knowledge of the medieval world to her exploration of the virtues and has created a work that both grips the imagination and stirs the heart. This book will be a resource and inspiration for years to come.

Sarah Clarkson, author of *Reclaiming Quiet* and *This Beautiful Truth*

In our current age, talking about vices and virtues may seem out of place, even weird. But Grace Hamman notes how the omnipresent vibrancy of a value-imbued medieval vocabulary challenges the modern reader to consider how deadened our language, and so our identity, has become by the emptiness of communication void of moral power. Hamman harkens back to the wisdom of a time in which the values of language reflected real habits and dispositions. In doing so, she calls for the rehabilitation of our own current language of the virtues so that we may pay more careful attention to our humanity made in the image of God. With her timely, beautiful, and compelling book, Hamman reminds us of a tried and telling truth: "Virtues are the fruit of well-ordered love." Indeed.

Dr. Carolyn Weber, professor at New College Franklin and award-winning author of *Sex and the City of God* and *Surprised by Oxford*, now a feature film

ASK *of* OLD PATHS

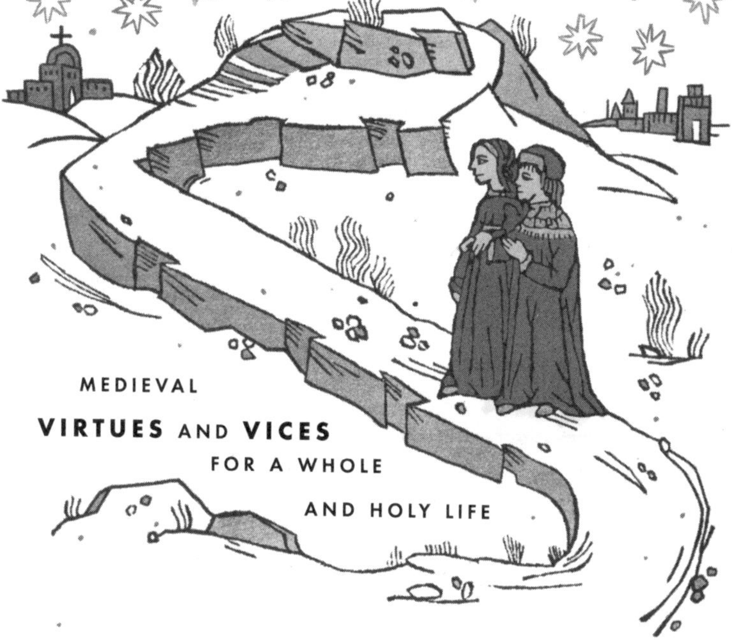

MEDIEVAL VIRTUES AND VICES FOR A WHOLE AND HOLY LIFE

GRACE HAMMAN

ZONDERVAN REFLECTIVE

Ask of Old Paths

Published by Zondervan, 3950 Sparks Drive SE, Suite 101, Grand Rapids, MI 49546, USA. Zondervan is a registered trademark of The Zondervan Corporation, L.L.C., a wholly owned subsidiary of HarperCollins Christian Publishing, Inc.

Requests for information should be addressed to customercare@harpercollins.com.

Zondervan titles may be purchased in bulk for educational, business, fundraising, or sales promotional use. For information, please email SpecialMarkets@Zondervan.com.

ISBN 978-0-310-16722-8 (audio)

Library of Congress Cataloging-in-Publication Data

Names: Hamman, Grace author
Title: Ask of old paths : medieval virtues and vices for a whole and holy life / Grace Hamman.
Description: Grand Rapids, Michigan : Zondervan Reflective, 2025.
Identifiers: LCCN 2025004997 (print) | LCCN 2025004998 (ebook) | ISBN 9780310167204 hardcover | ISBN 9780310167211 ebook
Subjects: LCSH: Literature, Medieval—History and criticism | Virtues in literature | Vices in literature | Art, Medieval | Virtues in art | Vices in art | LCGFT: Literary criticism | Art criticism
Classification: LCC PN682.V566 H36 2025 (print) | LCC PN682.V566 (ebook) | DDC 809/.93353—dc23/eng/20250508
LC record available at https://lccn.loc.gov/2025004997
LC ebook record available at https://lccn.loc.gov/2025004998

HarperCollins Publishers, Macken House, 39/40 Mayor Street Upper,
Dublin 1, D01 C9W8, Ireland (https://www.harpercollins.com)

Published in association with the literary agency of WordServe Literary Group, Ltd., www.wordserveliterary.com.

Cover design: Thinkpen Design
Cover art: © Morphart Creation / Shutterstock
Interior design: Sarah Johnson

Printed in the United States of America

25 26 27 28 29 LBC 7 6 5 4 3

For Margaret, Simon, and Constance

***

May you walk on old paths sure-footed in
the unconditional love of Jesus

CONTENTS

FOREWORD

Our God creates the world with words. "Let there be light, and there was light." Sounds like magic. Like a spell. The words are the things. But we no longer understand that. We are used to words being empty. Carcasses and husks.

In *Ask of Old Paths,* Grace Hamman injects life again into the dead bones of words. She plays with the puppets of the virtues and their strawmen vices until they come to life in her hands. We thought we knew what *love* meant, but not when we apply it to internet trolls and political opponents. Hamman knows we're uncomfortable considering pride and gluttony and lust as vices; aren't we past the reign of the Puritans? And she gets why contemporary readers may huff and snort at virtues such as meekness and chastity.

But she doesn't back down or let contemporary readers remain where they are. If they read *Ask of Old Paths,* they will accompany its author up a winding road that might feel a lot like the trail up Mount Purgatory on the return to Eden. We enter a medieval world with this Virgil, who never claims to be a virtuous paragon herself, and in fact, she confesses her own inadequacies in a way that becomes a model. The same mirror Hamman keeps jutting in front of our squinting faces is the one she holds before herself.

Books on virtue are *en vogue* right now. Apparently, they were in the fourteenth century too: "There exists so many books & treatises of vices and virtues . . . that any man will meet the end of his short life before he could study and read them all!"[1] If people

1. Cited from Henry Suso (d. 1366)

are writing books on virtues and vices, could it be the Holy Spirit telling us this is the medicine our sick culture requires?

Ask of Old Paths is a strong balm for our ailment. Hamman opens the book with a meditation on the meaning of the virtues and vices—the words themselves—as well as of "wholeness." How are we to heal without diagnosing rightly the sickness? And how are we to become well if we've forgotten what health looks like? For centuries, healthy meant wholeness, and holy and hallow, and . . . you have to read the book to follow all the paths of these words Hamman vivifies. We all desire wholeness, but sometimes it feels like a far-off dream or a faint memory.

The soul doctors in this book are not familiar with twenty-first century maladies, but the human heart has not changed since its creation. Their wisdom then is somehow more apt than the pseudo-cures of our present day. St. Thomas Aquinas, Bonaventure, Julian of Norwich, and medieval writers who are either anonymous or well-known only to scholars like Hamman speak from centuries before us into our time and place, and we'd do well to listen. To heed their knowledge of the virtues and vices that we might receive right remedy for our pains.

It's within this community of dead souls that we learn virtue is communal, not individualistic. From St. Catherine of Siena, we hear neighbors compared to a birth canal (spoiler alert!) by which our virtuous character may be born. And that virtues are not merely rules to be followed but habits to adopt and practices to live by. Hamman opens up abstract words like *temperance* and *avarice* and *meekness* to show us how we could be gluttons for words or those who cannot order our loves well or how meek could be powerful. She sits at the feet of Alasdair MacIntyre to explain his analogy that learning virtue is more akin to a child learning chess; you soon love the game for itself when you can play it well. The journey Hamman guides us through is a wandering one, but we are not alone.

In a culture where badness is uplifted everywhere, we need a community, but we also need a better way to see. You can choose the right books and try to choose the right schools for your kids and the right church for your family, but you turn a corner and there's a one-hundred-foot image of a mostly naked Victoria's Secret model. Or you're streaming *Babette's Feast* and super impressed with yourself for loving such a good film, and the movie is interrupted by an inane ad for Doritos followed by another commercial for Xanax. Can't we just replace all those images that clutter our brains and imprint themselves on us with better ones? I want to tear down the billboards of Kardashians and paste up Hamman's image from Giotto (1337) of Envy with a snake hissing from its mouth. Will the city council hear me out that we should remove the primary-colored mural of children dancing in a ring on the wall downtown with a painting of the unicorn in the lap of the Virgin Mary, reminding us of the beauty of chastity?

I often follow C. S. Lewis's admonition to read old books more than new books. But what if the new book is about old books? From *Ask of Old Paths*, it is evident that Hamman reads many old books. She has gathered them all together so that we may not travel this journey as individuals left to our own limited eyes, but that we can see by the light of these old souls. This is a new book steeped in lasting wisdom. We can more than make space for it on our shelves. In fact, I'll be so bold as to suggest that Lewis himself would recommend it.

Jessica Hooten Wilson
Fletcher Jones Chair of Great Books,
Pepperdine University

ACKNOWLEDGMENTS

Neither writing nor practicing virtues is a solitary endeavor. Thank you to my husband, Scott, who offers joy, honesty, encouragement, and a dash of much-needed excitement and chaos wherever he goes. Thank you to my parents, my trail guides in the virtues for my whole life. Thank you to Keely Boeving, beloved friend and brilliant agent. Thank you to Kyle Rohane, Alexis De Weese, Kim Tanner, and the whole Zondervan Reflective team for your patience, skill, and devotion to your craft. Thank you to my mother-in-law, Christie, for your faithful love and support. Thank you to my sister, Anna, and my brother, John, for your courage, delight, and love. Thank you to my beloved grandparents, John, Carol, and Ilene, for how you've lived the virtues in the lives of your family. Thank you to my dear children, joys of my life, primary birth canal for growing my own virtues. Thank you to the friends of my heart, Samantha, Chelsea, Goodie, Donica, and Marisa for seeing me and knowing me. Thank you to the best writing group in the land, Jessica Ward, Jessica Hines, and Lindsey Larre, each keen-eyed, generous, and wise. Thank you to the Monday night group for your glorious selves and for listening to my medieval jangling.

The ideas in this book would be unintelligible to me without the witness of your love.

Grace Hamman

First Sunday in Advent 2024

PREFACE
REVIVING THE GARDEN

> *"Where you tend a rose, my lad,*
> *A thistle cannot grow."*
>
> —Frances Hodgson Burnett,
> *The Secret Garden*

The antique words of old books shimmer with magic, though they were as ordinary then as ours today. Some of these enchanting words regretfully have faded from common use, like *bobbaunce* (ostentatious, swaggering behavior) or *wynne* (joy) or *welkyn* (sky). If you say them out loud, they still feel natural, English, but beautifully strange. Others are charming earlier forms of words we use all the time: *nosethirl* for nostril, literally nose passage, or *knyght,* which looks very familiar to us—a knight in shining armor! But in Middle English, every one of those sneaky consonants would have been pronounced: k-nee-gh-t, with the *gh* sounding like a German or Yiddish *ch*. Perhaps trickiest of all are the words we use in modernity, like *humilitee* or *prudence*; they look nearly the same as modern versions of a similar concept, yet they mean more. They operate more capaciously and powerfully.

Medieval people liked to compare the soul to a garden. Christ was the gardener who kept it, the guise that initially fooled and then thrilled Mary Magdalene after his resurrection. Sometimes even drawn in a gardener's floppy hat, Jesus pulled the weeds of one's vices and broke up the ground of the hardest hearts.[1] He lovingly harvested the fruits and nurtured the tender young sprouts of one's virtues. As I read Middle English works of poetry and devotion, I found that the medieval language of the virtues was like a garden gone wild after a rainstorm in July, filled with fruits and weeds and decaying organic matter, *so alive*. It wasn't always pleasant, not always intelligible, but pulsed with life, beauty, challenge.

In the medieval poems, plays, and pastoral writings that I studied in graduate school, many of the virtue words didn't map neatly onto what I thought they meant. I constantly danced around the strangeness of words like *avarice, meekness, sloth,* and *temperance*. They were not strange in the sense that I had never seen them before or that I did not know what they meant to twenty-first-century readers. But in their context, in the medieval poetry and contemplative writing that fascinated me, these words took on outlandish new forms. They made different shapes in my mind as I read them. They were heavy in their power to capture beauty and ugliness, weirdness and desire. How could I enter into this language? How could I understand it, in its nooks and crannies, its context so different from my own?

The vibrancy of these concepts confused me. For since childhood, I had recognized that the virtues were good but pretty dull. At least, I had always associated the language of "the virtues" with books about boring children. These books featured covers with pink, piglike, Eustace Scrubb–adjacent children who seemed likely to tattle on one another as they frolicked among flowers.

My own virtue vocabulary suddenly seemed desiccated, full

1. There are many drawings of Christ as a gardener, as in a manuscript now at the Bodleian Library in Oxford, MS Bodley 283, fol. 99v.

of shrunken, wilting words with shallow meanings. Glorious *prudence,* governor of the virtues, something akin to practical wisdom, faded into *prude,* the middle school insult. *Meekness,* a medieval virtue especially associated with Christ and Mary, became a crumbling tool of the patriarchy that made me crinkle my nose. The moral power seemed to have moved on and left these words behind.

Some of the virtues have never fully lost their appeal. I did want to be honest and brave, as most children do. Who doesn't feel awestruck when they consider the breathtaking courage of Saint Joan of Arc? And the practices of justice by Martin Luther King Jr. jolt us out of spiritual complacency. But these people seem special—called out of ordinariness. And with the notable exception of courage and occasionally justice, we rarely see the virtues in culturally relevant narratives.[2] When was the last time you watched a movie where the main character, especially a male main character, was notably patient or, worse, *meek,* two of the traditional virtues named by Christ himself?[3] Even (or especially) in Christianity, there are different standards for men and women. Good men practice courage; good women practice modesty. Historically, there have been different standards for racial categories as well: white people got to be generous and creative; people of color were urged toward humility and meekness. It all seemed tied to questionable-at-best, damaging-at-worst cultural norms. So up until I encountered the virtues in medieval books, my observations on them did not change much. My thoughts were pervaded by something like Shakespeare's famous lines in

2. It is often the opposite. In television, antiheroes rule the day (though to our limited credit, most of us don't particularly *want* to be Walter White or Tony Soprano).

3. I think the closest thing I've seen is the eponymous protagonist of *Ted Lasso.*

Twelfth Night: "She sat like patience on a monument / Smiling at grief."[4] This version of patience, like the virtues themselves, seemed passive, inauthentic.

Naturally, then, the vibrancy and ubiquity of these words in the medieval books I was reading caught my attention. The virtues were for everyone: ordinary people, not just saints, heroes, and government leaders in crisis. Far from being obscure, they were taught to the layfolk of the Middle Ages alongside the Apostle's Creed, the Lord's Prayer, and the Hail Mary. They were part of the bones of following Christ, of being human in the image of the Son of Man. What's more, the virtues in those texts were not boring but lively, particular, and often strange. Hedgehogs and snakes preached them, nail wounds and body parts conveyed them, Christ and Mary practiced them in utter fullness. The passivity I had mistaken for virtue would better be characterized as the absence of vice—which is not virtuous in its own right. I felt like I had missed something important. And I began to wonder if this medieval vocabulary of virtues and vices could help us where we are right now.

Why We Need the Language of the Virtues

If the modern language of the virtues feels more like dying potted plants than the wild, breathing garden it was in the Middle Ages, where did that life go? In American culture, the power in moral discourse seems to have moved into values language. Terms like *pro-choice, pro-gun,* or *anti-union,* when dropped into

4. William Shakespeare, *Twelfth Night,* II.IV.114–115.

a conversation, have atomic capacities of conveying who is evil and who is good, depending on the makeup of those conversing. The same is true of words like *Left* and *Right, Democrat* and *Republican, conservative* and *liberal*. Americans, as individuals or in groups like corporations, loudly proclaim support or resistance to LGBTQ+ people, to people of color, to women, to unborn babies, to free speech, to the Second Amendment, to teachers, to this and that candidate. It's not that having conversations about and making decisions based on what one values are bad; it's important to recognize, cherish, and act on those values. The problem is that values are an incomplete and inadequate way of determining the moral quality of actions and beliefs.

Values language often creates crude binaries. Take the political categories of left and right, traditionally set up in total opposition to each other. Values binaries erase the complexities of life together and of nuances in position. Contrary to how people use them, both right and left cover a wide range of beliefs, yet even those terms do not cover the full spectrum of beliefs people can hold. These binaries can also create false divisions between moral issues that should not be encouraged. For instance, rather than acknowledging that voters who want better, reasonable gun control and voters who oppose unrestricted abortion are both "pro-life" and may share goals, Christians on the political right and left skewer one another at the cost of a greater agreement on the value of each human created in the image of God.

Moreover, these moral binaries become a too easy, divisive litmus test: Are you on my team or the opposing team? Whenever my five-year-old son watches a new movie with us or hears about a classic movie he hasn't watched yet, he asks, "Who is the bad guy? Who is the good guy?" And though our vocabulary is a little more complex than his, adults do much the same when it comes to our values. This system works pretty well when it comes to *Star Wars*; it works less well when it comes to ordinary life. Most of us are neither as bad as Darth Vader nor as good as Leia (or Luke, post-whining stage). This demonization of the "other side" and idealization of "our side" blocks creative moral problem-solving and the possibility of transformation by creating a divide that no communication can cross. Even the most rabid values enemies may (and often do) share moral commitments that could be a source of problem-solving if we could jettison these crude binaries. We fail to ask seriously of opponents and their goals, Are they charitable? Are they just? Or even more usefully, Am I charitable? Am I just?

Another problem that surfaces for Christians is the relationship of values to loving response. Values by themselves do not automatically translate into meaningful and active responses of love. While proclaiming my values, I can virtue-signal what team I am on without changing any behavior. I can condemn fast fashion without curbing my habits of purchasing whatever cheaply made new thing I want to wear next. I can inveigh against abortion while voting against maternity leave reforms that would aid struggling women in carrying their babies to term and raising them. I become like those corporations who shill their Pride Month or Black History Month merchandise while exploiting and underpaying their employees, some of whom are likely Black or LGBTQ+. It's a yard-sign morality, a social media morality—what you publicly signal matters more than what you do.

In contrast, real virtues concern the habitual actions of a real person, a moral agent, not desires, signals, or even our teammates. When we empty our values language of our real habits and dispositions, we run into trouble. The fallout of our empty moral language has become abundantly clear in the last decade of public life. Americans have always been plagued by vicious candidates for public office, but we seem to have become even more strangely tolerant of bald-faced lies, unmasked arrogance, and cruelty. But who cares, as long as they're on the right team?

The Seven Capital Vices and Their Remedies

To rehabilitate the language of the virtues is to pay fresh attention to our creatureliness, to our identity as children of God, embodied souls, and thus to cultivate our actions and dispositions. Virtues are the fruit of well-ordered love. They are the habits of our values refined, reoriented, acted upon. This book wanders through the garden of the ancient tradition of virtue language called the seven capital vices and their remedies: the medieval word pictures and teachings on pride and humility; envy and love; wrath, patience, and meekness; avarice and mercy; sloth and fortitude; gluttony and abstinence; lust and chastity.[5]

I winced more than once as I typed that list. Sometimes these words feel unhelpfully old-fashioned. What person grappling with body image issues hears *gluttony* without a sinking dread? And not just the vices set my teeth on edge. What woman today sees *meekness* without a little shudder at the shadow of control? These words have at times been co-opted and wielded like weapons to enforce culturally "good" behavior at different points in

5. This is just one of the many traditions of virtue language out there, including the three theological virtues, the cardinal virtues, the seven deadly sins, and of course, the many secular virtues that are not neatly categorized, like ambition or industriousness. Note too that there are many potential remedy virtues in the tradition; these are "highlights."

history. Yet even though they are historically complicated words, I believe they are worth attending to—turning upside down and shaking like a piggy bank to see if anything of value emerges. I do not want to adopt these words wholesale, as if we were medieval ourselves, but to *think with them*, let them challenge me, and challenge them back. This book aims to tend to the language of the virtues, to give them back their life and color and otherworldly joy, by turning to medieval traditions of writing that have long been forgotten by all but scholars and confined to dusty corners of the library.

Each chapter will give some context on one of these vices and then dive deep into its "remedy," one or more of the virtues paired with it in medieval literature and pastoral writings. These virtues are called remedies not because they immediately fix the problem but because, like wholesome and medicinal plants in a garden, their cultivation begins to transform the person suffering under the oppressive habits we call vices.

The remedies aren't about "good behavior" or prudent life choices. The virtues are not about being a special individual who is better than other people. They are neither clumsy one-size-fits-all rules nor a dry works-righteousness perfectionism to be shoved upon others. In the practice of virtues, we become more wholly human, more ourselves as images of God. The seven capital vices and their remedies are a medieval guide on our long and winding journey into communal and individual wholeness, because you can't have one without the other.

What do I mean by wholeness? What even is a virtue? Let's explore the history of these deeply rooted and ancient ideas. But a last word of caution, too, before we clear out all these conceptual cobwebs. I am far from a perfect or even a good practitioner of these virtues; however, I am quite accomplished in the art of the vices. I can safely say that most of us are that way. Like other languages of healing (say, therapeutic language or biblical language), these powerful words easily wound and corrupt when they are wielded as diagnostic weapons against others rather than as formative and illuminating words as we peer into our own hearts and habits. In writing this book, I am trying to extract the log in my own eye (Matt. 7:3–5). Tend to the garden of your heart as we wander deeper into these concepts. This word-journey is for us, for you and me, in our pilgrimage in this life deeper into the kingdom of heaven.

CHAPTER ONE

WILT THOU BE MADE WHOLE?

Stondeth upon the weyes, and seeth and axeth
of olde pathes (that is to seyn, of olde sentences)
which is the goode way, / and walketh in that wey,
and ye shal fynde refresshynge for youre soules.

—Geoffrey Chaucer, *The Parson's Tale*

Stand at the crossroads and look,
and ask for the ancient paths,
where the good way lies; and walk in it,
and find rest for your souls.

—Jeremiah 6:16

Imagine yourself as a late fourteenth-century English person who celebrated the liturgical seasons of the medieval church. You laughed at and soberly absorbed Geoffrey Chaucer's marvelous new poems about pilgrimage, a popular kind of penitential spiritual formation. You lived alongside, quarreled with, and worshiped with your fellow parishioners, whether you lived in a sleepy agricultural village, a busy market town, or the hubbub of London itself. You fasted and reflected during Advent, feasted with raucous joy during the twelve days of Christmas, partied hard on Shrove Tuesday, and then observed "crabbed Lentoun" in pre-spring chill.[1] During Lent you prepared your heart for the great Paschal Feast, for Easter and its season of celebration. And unless you were an especially devout individual, you typically would have taken the Eucharist about once a year, in this season before Easter.[2]

To take Christ's body so seldom meant that a lot of serious preparation of the heart was to be made. With the assistance of your local priest, you readied yourself for the material presence of Jesus through the sacrament of penance. First, you reflected on your sins with contrition, the heartfelt regret that you have done things you ought not to have done, or left things undone that should have been done. Then, you confessed your sins to the

---

1. *Sir Gawain and the Green Knight* in *Poems of the Pearl Manuscript*, ed. Malcolm Andrew and Ronald Waldron (Exeter, UK: University of Exeter Press, 2007), l. 502.

2. For more on late medieval habits around Mass and receiving the Eucharist, see Eamon Duffy, *The Stripping of the Altars: Traditional Religion in England 1400–1380*, 2nd ed. (New Haven, CT: Yale University Press, 2005), ch. 3.

priest. Next, if you needed to do penance through prayer, pilgrimage, public apology, reparations to a wronged party, reconciliation with a neighbor, or something else entirely, you completed those tasks.[3] Finally, you took communion with a clear conscience that you were not disrespecting the true body of Jesus. Long before the dawn of therapy, people underwent this laborious process of developing self-knowledge and attempting to change their ways.

All kinds of practical matters intervened in this process of contrition and confession. What if you forgot a sin? Or what if you knew you struggled with something but didn't know the best way to combat it, or even how to describe it? Just like today, some priests were naturals at figuring out these problems and some needed a lot of help. In response to this situation, a popular genre of writing sprang up: spiritual treatises meant to help priests aid their parishioners in examining their conscience and for laypeople themselves to explore the moral quandaries of the soul and body. As one Middle English translation of a much-read book of contemplation by Henry Suso (d. 1366) explained, "There exists so many books & treatises of vices and virtues & of diverse doctrines, that any man will meet the end of his short life before he could study and read them all!"[4] These books, intended for use in pastoral and

3. The sacrament of penance followed the same basic pattern, yet it varied wildly with time, place, and quality of priest. To learn more, see Duffy, *Altars*, 54–60; and Thomas Tentler's massive *Sin and Confession on the Eve of the Reformation* (Princeton, NJ: Princeton University Press, 1977).

4. "There beeth so manye bokes & tretees of vyces and vertues & of dyverse doctrynes, thar this schort lyfe schalle rathere have anenende of anye manne thane he maye owthere studye or rede hem." From the Middle English translation of the *Orologium sapientiae*, by Henry Suso, ed. K. Horstman, *Anglia*, X (1888), 328, 22, found in the introduction to Richard Lavynham, *A Litil Tretys*, ed. J. P. W. M. van Zutphen (Institutum Carmelitanum, 1956), x. Unless otherwise noted, I have lightly translated all Middle English quotations into modern English.

contemplative practices, often described the sacraments as well as the vices people were likely to succumb to, or the virtues that would help them become more like Christ. The vices they described were consistent: those seven capital vices, accompanied by a varying list of their remedies. These pastoral materials influenced and were influenced by poetry, contemplative literature, and plays in popular medieval culture. And this collection of motley medieval materials—the poetry, contemplative literature, plays, priests' handbooks, and layfolk's books of spiritual formation—is what I will explore as I tend to the garden of virtue language.[5]

The concept of vices and virtues already had a long history before appearing in the poetry, plays, and pastoral materials of the late Middle Ages, despite the fact that the Bible does not explicitly mention the seven capital vices or their remedies. Sometimes Christians don't like virtue language because the virtues feel like an extrabiblical imposition, something people made up to get others to act the way they think is good. But we run into all kinds of problems when we think of the important things in the Bible as only those that are spelled out explicitly: The Bible also doesn't systematically lay out the Trinity or many other important Christian doctrines and traditions that the early church developed and articulated through prayer and pastoral guidance. The virtues are one helpful way the historical church thought about spiritual transformation and growth, of the fruits of the Holy Spirit and the life of love.

5. Many of these pastoral works translate or cobble together older sources. This book makes no attempt to trace their origins or the originality of the images, metaphors, and comparisons, most of which are reused and recycled throughout medieval writings. The materials used in this book are mostly Middle English and Latin works and represent a fraction of the wide range of medieval content on the virtues and vices.

In the Christian tradition, two main paths of virtue language have crossed, converged, and diverged throughout the years. One path began with Plato, Aristotle, and the ancient Greek philosophers, roughly four hundred years before the birth of Christ. Aristotle (d. 322 BC) in particular developed a robust theory of virtue, oriented toward the good of the *polis*, the city. He probed the four cardinal virtues of prudence, justice, temperance, and fortitude.[6] The Romans, too, liked these ideas. Yet the life of virtue was reserved exclusively for male citizens of the city-state; Aristotle did not believe women and enslaved people could fully practice the virtues. For obvious reasons, this does not sit well with us.

Another story of the virtues and vices began in the desert of Egypt, with the birth of Christian monasticism. About three hundred years or so after the death of Christ, people like Saint Anthony (d. 356) started to withdraw to the desert to build communities based on a life of ascetism and vows of poverty. In that process, others like Evagrius Ponticus, John Cassian, and Amma Theodora compiled pastoral aids for resisting the temptations of the desert.

I grew up in the Sonoran Desert, far from the Egypt of early monasticism. But I know the desert well. By its nature, a desert strips all things to their bones. Picked dry, bleached out, solitary—even the soul experiences these conditions. The desert is cleansing, even beautiful, but harsh. The Desert Fathers and

---

6. Read Aristotle's *Nicomachean Ethics* for yourself—it's not as daunting as it may seem! Jennifer Herdt helpfully introduces Aristotle's writing on the virtues and his legacy in *Putting on Virtue: The Legacy of the Splendid Vices* (Chicago: University of Chicago Press, 2008), ch. 1. For anyone wishing to discover the importance of Aristotle's theories of the virtues and on traditions of moral language, read Alasdair MacIntyre, *After Virtue: A Study in Moral Theory*, 3rd ed. (Notre Dame: University of Notre Dame Press, 2007).

Mothers knew that when you retreat from society into the literal or metaphorical desert of solitude, from the ever-changing company and views and products and foods, you are left with your own thoughts. You are faced with the temptations deep inside you. Before the desert, you may have managed to hide these thoughts, feelings, and actions from yourself—or at least obscure them from other people. In their attention to the soul in the desert as it becomes exposed to itself, the Desert Mothers and Fathers listed these temptations and their characteristics in the early days of the format we now call the seven capital vices: pride or vainglory, envy, wrath, sloth, lust, gluttony, and greed or avarice.[7]

These seven capital vices are not quite the same concept as the seven deadly sins.[8] *Capital* comes from the Latin word for head, *caput*, as in fountainhead or beginning (think of a capital letter at the beginning of a sentence). It's not that this list contains exhaustive detail of every possible vice, nor is it that once these vices are committed, they automatically damn you. This list consists of the roots, the sources, of all the vicious actions that occur to the perpetually inventive human.

This catalog of vices emerged from pastoral care—that is, from the leaders learning how to spiritually guide and truly love the men and women in their communities. As part of their work

---

7. For a fuller account of this history and development, read Rebecca Konyndyk DeYoung's wonderfully clear and accessible introduction in *Glittering Vices: A New Look at the Seven Deadly Sins and Their Remedies*, 2nd ed. (Grand Rapids: Brazos, 2020).

8. "Deadly sins" lead inevitably to damnation if unconfessed, according to historical theology, and the term is "rarely, if at all, applied to the cardinal sins before the fourteenth century," Morton Bloomfield, *The Seven Deadly Sins: An Introduction to the History of a Religious Concept, with Special Reference to Medieval English Literature* (Michigan State University Press, 1952, reprint 1967), 43–44.

as shepherds, these thinkers crafted this list to focus on people's actions and common obstacles we face as we learn to follow Christ, and ways to combat those temptations. Some of the great pastoral thinkers of the early Middle Ages, like Pope Gregory the Great and Saint Benedict of Nursia, further developed the traditional vices alongside some opposing virtues and their roles in lives of community, especially monastic communities.[9] Into the Middle Ages, writers and theologians paired remedies—virtues from scriptural sources, particularly the Beatitudes, Paul's letters, and the life of Christ himself—with the ubiquitous list of vices: humility; love; patience or meekness; fortitude or strength; mercy; abstinence and other virtues of temperance; and chastity.

Medieval theologians like Saint Thomas Aquinas (d. 1274) took these pastoral tools of thinking about vice, virtue, habits, and human behavior and juxtaposed them to some of the more theoretical ideas about the life of human happiness postulated by Aristotle and his medieval Arabic commentators.[10] By the fourteenth century in England, scholars, priests, poets, contemplatives, and ordinary laypeople were all wrestling with these ideas in their daily lives, using them to think about their own behavior, what they owed to one another as brothers and sisters in Christ, and how their lives might be transformed. This medieval

9. See Gregory the Great, *Moralia in Job*, ed. and trans. John Henry Parker (London: J. G. F. and J. Rivington, 1844), book XXXI, accessed September 20, 2023, http://www.lectionarycentral.com/GregoryMoralia/Book31.html. See also Saint Benedict of Nursia, *The Rule of St. Benedict*, trans. Leonard J. Doyle (Collegeville, MN: Liturgical Press, 1948), accessed September 20, 2023, https://www.gutenberg.org/files/50040/50040-h/50040-h.htm.

10. A lot of Aristotle's writing comes to us only through the preservation of the Islamic world. That's another hugely fascinating story!

process of intentionally weeding out vices and cultivating virtues reminds us that this practice of spiritual formation is eminently practical, teaching us about being a human with other humans in community and about being in relationship with Christ.

Hale, Healed, Hallowed, Holy, Whole

Our virtues do not earn Christ's love. Instead, while we were sinners, Christ loved us and died for us (Rom. 5:8). His love gives us the freedom to participate in our own process of becoming whole—an ongoing process into eternity. In the gospel of John, Jesus goes up to Jerusalem. By a healing pool he meets a man who has been ill for a very long time. Jesus then asks the man a famous question. Modern translations like the NRSV render it "Do you want to be made well?" (John 5:6). The man explains to Jesus that he can't get into the water fast enough; someone else always gets there first, and he has no one to help him into the healing pool. Jesus replies, "Stand up, take your mat and walk" (John 5:8). And the man is made well. The Middle English Bible translated Christ's question as "Wolt thou be maad hool? [Do you will to be made whole?]."[11]

In this encounter, medieval theologians like Aquinas traced the total salvation of humankind by Jesus, and humanity's subsequent cooperation with God in their sanctification.[12] Christ

11. Middle English translation of the Vulgate, *Wycliffe's Bible*, ed. Josiah Forshall and Frederic Madden (Oxford, UK: Oxford University Press, 1850). Other older English Bibles like the King James and the Douay-Rheims also use *whole*.

12. Thomas Aquinas, *Commentary on John*, trans. Fabian R. Larcher O.P., ed. The Aquinas Institute (Green Bay, WI: Aquinas Institute, 2013), C. 5 L. 1.

asks if we want to be healed. And he heals in the work of salvation. And then in obedience, as part of our healing, we pick up our mats and take those surprising steps forward. Those actions constitute the curious paradox of the Christian way: As we seek to follow Jesus, our actions of love that constitute our ongoing transformation are both graced and our own, all at once. In the Middle English translation of this passage, "well" and even more so "whole" ultimately imply something beyond simply "healed"—they offer a vision of particular fullness of life. This is what theologians have called sanctification: the process of becoming a more whole human being, becoming more like Jesus.

In college I had an unusual encounter with the word *whole*. I took a class called History of the English Language. The professor was an ancient, crotchety man, the kind of professor who loved to harvest exam answers from footnotes in the textbook. His final assignment for the class was a three- to-five-page essay on the history of *one word*. I considered choosing the buoyant, glittering *glorious*. I pondered something provocative, like a swear word, or worse, *moist*. Anticlimactically, I chose—you guessed it—*whole*.[13]

Whole led me down a fascinating rabbit hole of language, back thousands of years before English was a language, to the common primeval source of many European languages that scholars call Indo-European. Like a dinosaur bone found underneath a mall parking lot, many of the words we use casually today contain fossilized remnants of the past. *Whole*'s Indo-European root was something similar to *hal*. From *hal* emerges many words:

13. I was intrigued by the silent *w*, which ended up being less exciting than I thought: The *w* apparently lingers as a bizarre artifact of a short-lived, historical pronunciation of the word as "wole" (much later than these *h* beginnings!).

whole itself, but also *health, heal,* and *hale,* like in the old saying "hale and hearty."[14] The word *hail* (not the weather condition) also springs from this ancient word-well: To "hail" the king is to honor the king by wishing him wholeness and health. And finally, *holy* and *hallow* belong to this word family. When Christ asks the man, *Do you want to be whole?* he means this whole bundle. Being made whole is a package that includes healing our bodies and our neighbors, cultivating holiness, hallowing the name of God, and nurturing the haleness of the heart. This process extends beyond time and our present bodies into eternity.

The Middle English Bible curiously translates Christ's command to the man as "Ryse up, taak thi bed, and wandre [Rise up, take thy bed, and wander]." *Wander* could mean, in Middle English, straightforward walking. But it also held all the connotations it has today: meandering, exploring, trying out a new road. That translation reminds me that practicing the virtuous life includes mistakes, setbacks, reorienting, road maps, and guides and fellow pilgrims along the way. Our wandering is not aimless but disciplined by our love and the love of God.

Humans are creatures of desire. We are oriented toward seeking and giving love as our ultimate purpose, what the ancients called a *telos,* or end. The great African bishop Saint Augustine of Hippo (d. 430) famously wrote of this driving, teleological desire at length in his *Confessions.* Present-day philosopher James K. A. Smith comments on Augustine's insight: "The question isn't *whether* you will love something as ultimate; the question is

---

14. *Oxford English Dictionary,* "whole" (adj., n., & adv.), Etymology, June 2024, https://doi.org/10.1093/OED/9222636923; Joseph Bosworth, "hál" (adj.), *Bosworth Toller's Anglo-Saxon Dictionary,* ed. Thomas Northcote Toller, Christ Sean, and Ondřej Tichy (Faculty of Arts, Charles University, 2014), accessed July 8, 2024, https://bosworthtoller.com/18028.

what you will love as ultimate."[15] For Aristotle, that ultimate end of desire, the goal of human striving, was the good of the *polis*, the city, but as Christians, we believe the ultimate fulfilling of longing and loving is the kingdom of heaven and seeing the face of God at last. Therefore, we recognize that true wholeness, the utter fulfilling of our love, comes only after we die. But here and now, we have pieces of it as our character becomes more oriented toward the vision of the kingdom of heaven, as we have a part to play in restoring wholeness to our fallen world (hence our petition, "Thy will be done, on Earth as it is in Heaven"). We wander toward wholeness as we see it in its limited, tantalizing glimpses in Christ's life on earth, in the Sermon on the Mount, in Paul's letters to the church, and in the writings and lives of those more advanced in holy wandering than ourselves, past and present. Sanctification requires picking up my mat and wandering, practicing, experimenting, walking, by the grace of God.

Creatures of Habit

We need the virtues because we cannot talk or wish ourselves into this wholeness. This is because we are creatures, not disembodied minds or abstract wills. We come in a soul-body package that can't be separated until we die, and even then, in some mysterious way, this separation is not permanent.

Creature, like *whole*, is another funny word. A creature is a life created. It was only after reading Middle English that I mentally

---

15. James K. A. Smith, *You Are What You Love: The Spiritual Power of Habit* (Grand Rapids: Brazos, 2016), 10.

connected the word *creature* to *creation*. The medieval English mystical writer Margery Kempe (d. 1438) referred to herself almost exclusively as "this cretur" in her first-person account of her encounters with God in fifteenth-century Europe.[16] At first, this elocution may strike the reader as unnerving or just odd. Why would a woman, writing in a genre now tied deeply to ideas about transcending the body and meeting the divine, place such emphasis on this word that also applies to animals or to monsters—in other words, to the embodied? It is because Margery was perpetually recognizing and remembering herself as God's own creation.

In my creaturely fullness, I am particular, embodied, ensouled. I emerge from another embodied, ensouled creature. I also like *creature* because in our modern English, it connotes wildness. It groups me with owls, octopi, and spiders. When I had my first child, I caught a glimpse of my creatureliness like never before. My baby came out of my body with a lot of blood, and this tiny creature, human yet also a yowling, naked cub, then fed from my body. I felt like a wild animal in the woods. Years later this same creature asked me penetrating, impossible questions like, "Could Jesus breathe underwater?" We cannot divorce the body and the soul. To think of myself as a creature like Margery means I come from somewhere, I am going somewhere, in certain company, in particular places. My wandering into wholeness as a creature will necessarily include body, mind, and soul.

Because transformation involves our hearts, minds, and bodies, we are creatures of habit. Both virtues and vices are habits, things we *do* with our body or mind over and over until they

16. Margery Kempe, *The Book of Margery Kempe*, ed. Lynn Staley (Kalamazoo, MI: Medieval Institute Publications, 1996).

become part of our character. Sometimes virtues begin as divine gifts—as the free charity of God. Sometimes they are "fake it till you make it," unnatural or exterior to us at first, and then the more we do them, the more they become part of who we are. Often it's a combination. Habits can be practiced and cultivated, or disrupted and destroyed over time and repetition, as anyone knows who has tried to follow an exercise regimen or who has learned to read. A virtue is "an excellent and stable quality of the soul that enables a person to act well regarding some kind of activity."[17] Christians specifically believe that a virtue enables a person to *love* well in thought and act.

For us embodied creatures, love can be confusing and difficult. We have the gift of natural loves, set in us in our very creation, loves that help us to especially love our friends and family or to take care of our bodies by eating, drinking, and sleeping. Yet we can love such gifts excessively or deficiently, depending on the context. We see it all the time in broken families, abused or neglected bodies, catastrophes in conflict and war. A vice is a practice that corrodes and obscures our identities as images of God, a practice in which our love is misdirected, excessive, or deficient, generally out of joint. Vices corrupt our humanity and twist our natural loves. A virtue, on the other hand, is a habit that makes us more human, more conformed to the image of God that is our deepest identity. Saint Thomas Aquinas writes that "virtue designates a certain kind of perfection of a power," meaning that in its practice, a virtue moves our will or our intellect or both toward wholeness.[18]

---

17. Craig A. Boyd and Kevin Timpe, *The Virtues: A Very Short Introduction* (Oxford: Oxford University Press, 2021), 4.

18. Thomas Aquinas, *Treatise on the Virtues*, trans. John A. Oesterle (Notre Dame: University of Notre Dame Press, 1984), 51 (*ST* I-II.55.2.r).

As habits, vices and virtues are stable—that is, in their practice, they become part of our character. We have all met individuals uniquely brave, bitterly angry, remarkably loyal, or eaten up by envy. We recognize a virtue or vice in someone because it characterizes their typical response to challenging situations. These people aren't loyal once, brave once, or wrathful or envious once.

Humans learn virtues just as we learn other crafts of excellence, like reading or playing basketball. At first, a child can read for only a short period of time, with a Bob Book or Dr. Seuss, but as they practice and practice, they progress to reading *Charlotte's Web*, then further until they can pick up and enjoy *The Brothers Karamazov*. This practice of habituation belongs to activities of the body, the mind, and the heart. If I tried to run right now, I would make it a dreadful five minutes before giving up. But some people train up to doing ultramarathons. Running has become a habit for them. The repetition of a habit increases ease and skill.

I assume, not being a marathoner myself, that one can run a lot of marathons and not do them for the love of running but for other perks, like staying in shape or getting one of those circle stickers with "26.2" for the back of one's car. One difference between a virtue and a mere habit is the love of the practice itself. It involves both capacity and desire, body and spirit. The famous moral philosopher Alasdair MacIntyre compares learning the virtues to a child learning chess.[19] The adult teaching the child chess will explain moves, play with him, and reward him for trying and for well-done moves. These rewards could be candy or affirmation. The child at first plays for these rewards because chess itself is challenging and not as immediately enjoyable as

19. MacIntyre, *After Virtue*, 188.

Candy Land. But as the child masters the game, the game itself becomes the reward. The child learns to love chess for its own sake. Through practicing virtue, we learn to love virtuous action not for the rewards it gains us but for the virtue itself.

A truly virtuous act is done not for an extrinsic reward but for its own intrinsic sake, because it is right and oriented toward love of God or love of neighbor. And because virtue is a habit, individual acts can look or even be virtuous without the agent herself possessing a virtuous character. Take the classic example of courage, sometimes known as fortitude. Aquinas writes of fortitude as what enables a person to remove an obstacle standing in the way of love. The traditional example of courage is a soldier fighting for his country. But even this is complex: A soldier in World War I may go over the top of his trench in warfare, an act of undoubted bravery. But he himself may not be a courageous person or practicing true courage. He could be just following orders because he does not want to be shot for desertion. He may be chasing a thrill of adrenaline or pridefully looking to boost his reputation among his fellow soldiers. Or he may just want to slaughter Germans. A man rescuing a cat from a tree might be more truly virtuous.[20] As a result, observation alone can't always tell us whether someone is truly courageous, or just seeking glory, or only enjoying an adrenaline rush. In real life the distinctions between extrinsic and intrinsic motivations are often messy and unclear.

Another mistake I had made about the virtues was thinking about them as individual, as belonging to individuals and being individual in themselves. But we are communal creatures, social

---

20. See C. S. Lewis's famous example in *Mere Christianity* (San Francisco, CA: HarperSanFrancisco, 2001), 91.

animals by our nature. The very development and practice of virtue is a collective labor of beauty and struggle. Saint Catherine of Siena (d. 1380) writes, "Your neighbors are the channel through which all your virtues are tested and come to birth, just as the evil give birth to all their vices through their neighbors." Neighbors as a birth canal! No one is humble, just, hopeful, or patient in a vacuum: "You test the virtue of patience in yourself when your neighbors insult you. Your humility is tested by the proud, your faith by the unfaithful, your hope by the person who has no hope. Your justice is tried by the unjust, your compassion by the cruel, and your gentleness and kindness by the wrathful."[21]

Or, unfortunately, you practice your impatience and anger when something does not go your way. You have endless opportunities for sneering or judging when faced with incompetent people. You train yourself in lust as you objectify bodies of real neighbors.

On the flip side, you become patient by watching or being on the receiving end of someone else's patience. You practice hope by hoping with another hopeful person. Becoming habituated in virtue requires teachers and mentors. We begin to recognize courage by looking at the lives, choices, and words of people like Dr. King or Dietrich Bonhoeffer or your big sister or college roommate. We can learn humility at the feet of Saint Francis of Assisi or Julian of Norwich or your fourth-grade teacher or grandfather. We love our neighbor as ourselves in watching our neighbors, in learning from them, in discovering the love of God together. Sanctification is deeply cooperative and communal.

---

21. Saint Catherine of Siena, *The Dialogue*, trans. Suzanne Noffke, O.P. (New York: Paulist, 1980), 38–39.

The Virtues Are Not One-Size-Fits-All

It is significant that the virtues are not rules, laws, or even guidelines, but habits of creatures oriented toward love of God and neighbor. As a result, the virtues are not one-size-fits-all. They are incredibly flexible, diverse, contextual, and sometimes hidden from plain sight. Some of the greatest moments of humility in a person's life will remain forever unseen, even by those closest to that person. An act may require great courage and go unnoticed. Conversely, sometimes practicing justice will require a lot of cage-rattling and gain much attention.

The virtues contract and expand to fit individual lives and points in history. Some virtues do not change too much over thousands of years—a soldier in combat defending his people has been an emblem of courage for a very long time. But a corporate whistleblower exposing injustice at the cost of her job would baffle a sixth-century monk. A six-year-old would hopefully never be in the context of going over the top of a trench, but I've known some courageous six-year-olds and have learned from them. Historical and individual contexts matter.

Because the virtues are not a set of moral laws, we can learn from medieval folks' depiction and usage of the virtues, despite not living in a medieval world. Their thoughts and images of the virtues can help us riddle out such unmedieval problems as our conduct on social media and voting rights. And thankfully, in the great freedom of the virtues, we do not have to apply the same logic as medieval people did when thinking about the shape of the virtuous life. Many things that looked like virtue to them I would vigorously resist as virtuous—for instance, a woman staying with her abusive partner in the name of patience or chastity. Some might mistakenly call this moral relativism. But again, the virtues have never been a set of moral precepts, even from their scriptural roots. Like a story, they are always contextualized in the time, place, and community in which they are practiced, by necessity.[22]

The virtues' inherent flexibility and contextual nature also give grace in regard to one of the apparent injustices of human life: that we do not all have the same gifts, whether those are spiritual or physical. On a physical level, we know this to be true. I have not practiced the grueling habituation of LeBron James or Katie Ledecky or Beyoncé or Yo-Yo Ma. But even if I tried to, I would not be as excellent as them in their crafts of basketball, swimming, performing, and playing the cello. I did all right in high school swim. But I simply do not have the physical gifts necessary to be an Olympic gold medalist. Yet I am still called to take care of my body through cultivating habits of exercise and eating well.

There are equally virtuosos of the virtues. I may never be as kind as Fred Rogers or as full of charity as Saint Therese of Lisieux. But I love and admire them; I take courage from them and imitate them. These differences in our predilections and giftings in no way determine our value to God or our salvation. Saint Catherine of Siena asked God why he made some virtues easy for some people and very difficult for others. She recorded these words from God:

> Why do I give this person one virtue and that person another, rather than giving them all to one person? It is true that all the virtues are bound together, and it is impossible to have

22. See MacIntyre, *After Virtue*, ch. 15.

> one without having them all. But I give them in different ways so that one virtue might be, as it were, the source of all the others. So to one person I give charity as the primary virtue, to another justice, to another humility, to another a lively faith or prudence or temperance or patience, and to still another courage. . . . Through her love of that virtue she attracts the other virtues to herself, since they are all bound together in loving charity.[23]

Our different skill sets and what we find simpler or what comes more naturally to us becomes a beautiful way into community, into loving one another, into appreciating each other more fully. The toe and the spleen are different, yet they each contribute to the wholeness of the body of Christ. Of course, this metaphor doesn't quite work in full because while the toe and spleen are made for different practices, we are all called to patience, to justice, and to love. Yet our practices will necessarily look different from one another in the unfolding story of our lives.

Wandering After Wholeness

Is all of this, as Nietzsche would argue, just another form of slavery? Is it all just another guilt-laden way to make us feel bad so we will fall in line, whatever that looks like in our historical moment? Or are the virtues a bootstraps gospel, a Pelagian tit-for-tat exchange? *I'll be good, God, and then you'll give me what I want.* Are we just reheating the ever-present medieval anxiety of *don't*

23. Catherine of Siena, *Dialogue*, 57.

miss a sin for fear of offending the Lord? The language of the virtues and vices can easily devolve into these latter two in particular.

Yet for me the virtues boil down to Christ's question: *Do you want to be whole?* What do I desire? I don't want to be patient because I've been told it's the right thing to do. I want to be patient because I recognize that when I am patient, I love my husband and children more wholly as themselves in all their complexity and beauty. I do not want to be humble because it's the right thing to do. I want to be humble because I want to genuinely plumb the depths of my creatureliness. I do not want to be just simply so that I avoid hell. I want to be just because my injustice creates little hells for myself and for other people. When Jesus asks, "Do you want to be made well?" I answer yes. I long to be made whole. I long for other people to be made whole.

Meditating on the vices and virtues will not "fix" us or even make us more virtuous. A lot of holy people out there aren't exactly sure how to define some of these words. But these words aid us on our way. My tendency—and I suspect yours as well—is to continually justify my actions, craft them into the most reasonable, the most understandable thoughts and actions possible, even when I know what I did was not great. In considering the vices, we begin to know ourselves better: our motivations, our failures, and our special temptations. Understanding the vices helps us to move past the project of self-justification and into our truer and preexisting justification through Jesus. We excavate our motives out of the darkness in which we bury them, and confess. In that movement, we participate in our ongoing sanctification in Christ. We begin to know ourselves as weak and in need of mercy and help and to celebrate how we are treasured in our valuable limitations. Confession always comes before transformation.

As for the virtues? I think of Philippians 4:8 (NIV): "Finally, brothers and sisters, whatever is true, whatever is noble, whatever is right, whatever is pure, whatever is lovely, whatever is admirable—if anything is excellent or praiseworthy—think about such things." Thinking critically about the remedies is worthwhile even if only for admiring something difficult, bizarre, and often lovely. But it does more than that: The virtues can give us a vocabulary, guide rails, pilgrim friends. Diving into their images, pausing on their beauty, and soaking in their strangeness can breathtakingly sharpen and direct our desires in expansive, creative, divine love. For love grows as understanding grows.

In the end, these are deep waters, and we are only treading the surface. At the conclusion of his marvelous *Confessions*, Augustine muses on the mystery of the human heart and its transformations: "What human can empower another human to understand these things?"[24] He concludes that we must keep asking, seeking, knocking at Christ's door, and only then will we receive, find, and walk in.

In the grace of Jesus Christ, I pick up my mat. Let us wander after wholeness, though the road be long and strange.

---

24. Saint Augustine of Hippo, *Confessions*, trans. Maria Boulding, O.S.B. (New York: Vintage Books, 1997), 342.

CHAPTER TWO

PRIDE AND HUMILITY: LION AND CHILD

There is a progress which consists in coming downstairs all the time, till at last we reach that level of truth from which we can say, "Out of the depths have I cried unto Thee, O Lord," and regain the sense of proportion that humanity has lost in respect of God.

—Evelyn Underhill

"Truly I tell you, unless you change and become like children, you will never enter the kingdom of heaven. Whoever becomes humble like this child is the greatest in the kingdom of heaven."

—Matthew 18:3–4

In encountering the popular medieval imagery of the Tree of Vices and the Tree of Virtues, you almost feel like a wanderer in a dream or a woodcutter's son in a fairy tale. Two trees stand in a grove found only in the pages of crackling vellum manuscripts. Snakes sinuously entwine the trunk of the first tree. Small dragons cling to the fruits that emerge from the branches. As your eye travels down to the roots, in a nightmarish twist, you realize the roots are actually a woman, dressed in red, crowned in glory. She is Pride, cunning queen of the vices, and each leaf of this strange tree bears the name of another vice: wrath, gluttony, envy, down the list. (See images on pp. 26–27.)

The tree on the right is flanked by angels with thin, gleaming halos. Its fruits, labeled in tiny Latin inscriptions as different virtues, upturn to heaven as they grow from the trunk of the tree. The tree flowers magnificently at the top, the bloom no other than Love himself, Christ, with hand outstretched in blessing. This tree springs from the body of an androgynous figure sketched plainly in black, lacking the reds and greens of the rest of the scene: Humility.[1]

Roots and foundations are the common imagery of both humility and pride.[2] Pride's foundational role in the vices is commonly known and accepted. "Pride goeth before the fall," we say,

---

1. Tree of Vices and Tree of Virtues, *Speculum virginum*, ca. first quarter of thirteenth century, Walters Art Museum, Baltimore, M.S. W 72 26 v & 26 r.

2. *ST* II-II.161.5.ad2., Thomas Aquinas writes that if the life of virtue were a building, humility would be the foundation.

even non-Christians unknowingly paraphrasing Proverbs (16:18 KJV). We may not know exactly what that means, but we do know it. While we all struggle to a greater or lesser extent with different vices—for some of us, envy is a greater temptation than sloth, or lust than avarice—pride is universal, and we will explore its universality in the following section. But why humility? More specifically, why isn't *love* the foundation of all virtues?[3]

In modernity, humility is the bench player in public discussions of virtue. Bench players come in handy at times, but management is not putting them on any stadium-adorning banners, and no one buys their jerseys. When I google *humility*, it quickly becomes clear that we're not all that sure why humility is important. One list of "humble quotes" vaguely argues that humility is important because it is "inspiring"; a business website says it matters because humility persuades people to follow you! Deep down, I suspect we all have a bit of the eighteenth-century Enlightenment philosopher David Hume (d. 1776) in us. He writes that humility and its fellow "monkish virtues" "*serve to no manner of purpose*; neither to advance a man's fortune in the world, nor render him a more valuable member of society; neither qualify him for the entertainment of company, nor increase his power of self-enjoyment."[4] Here's Hume recast into modern language: Humility doesn't seem all that personally helpful in the competitive atmosphere of business or school or work. If I don't totally back myself, who will? Humility was useless in the sophisticated drawing rooms of the

3. In reading medieval literature, I was so confounded by humility that I wrote an entire dissertation on it. See Grace Hamman, *Matter of Meekness: Reading Humility in Late Medieval England*, unpublished dissertation (Proquest, 2019).

4. David Hume, *An Enquiry Concerning the Principles of Morals*, ed. J. B. Schneewind (Indianapolis, IN: Hackett Publishing Company, 1983), 73, italics in the original.

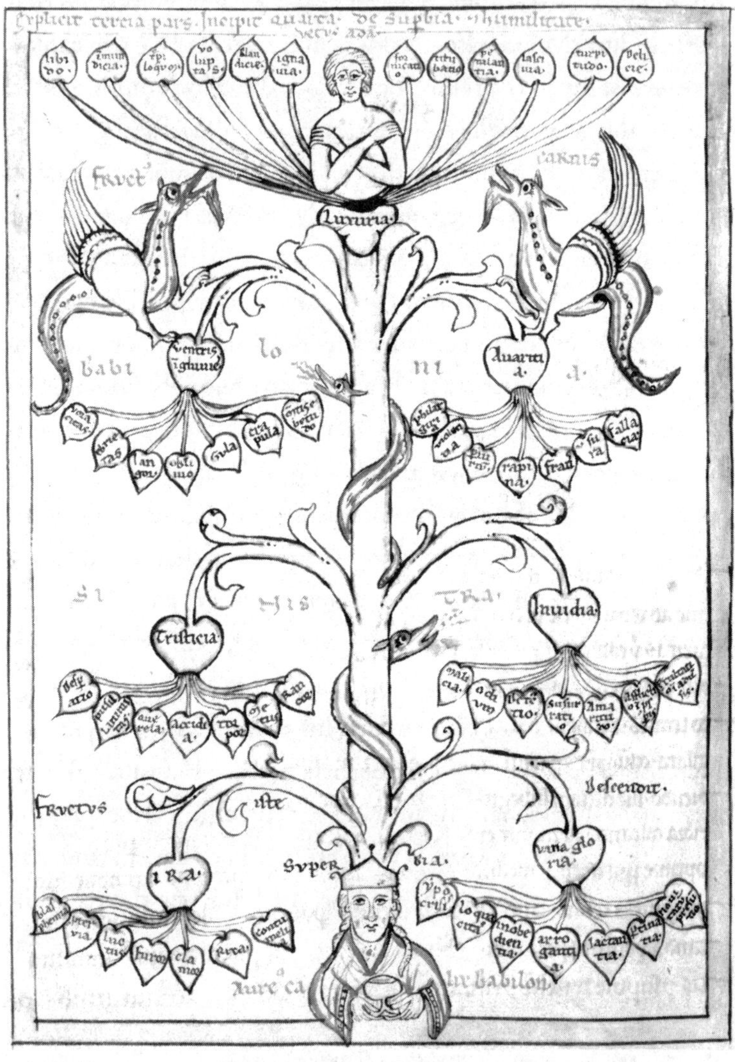

The Tree of Vices, *Speculum Virginum*, manuscript illumination, ca. first quarter of the thirteenth century, Walters MS W 72, fol. 26v, Walters Art Museum, Baltimore. The Walters Art Museum/CC0

The Tree of Virtues, *Speculum Virginum,* manuscript illumination, ca. first quarter of the thirteenth century, Walters MS W 72, fol. 26r, Walters Art Museum, Baltimore. The Walters Art Museum/CC0

Enlightenment where clever people figured out the way the world should work. It still seems superfluous in the places where the best thought, the best athleticism, the best art, the most pleasurable experiences are coaxed into being. Theologian Jane Foulcher notes the irony that "in Western culture, the word *humility* is used most comfortably as a way of portraying an individual's gracious bearing of success."[5] If we continue the sports metaphor, of course one would prefer the superstars of the virtues: love, faith, courage. Their utility is obvious.

Yet one of the more outrageous things medieval people teach on the virtues is that none of the superstars are worth much outside of the practices and character of humility. Pope Gregory the Great (d. 604) preached, "Whoever gathers all the virtues without humility, carries as it were dust into the wind."[6] Severed from the roots of the living vine of humility, each virtue swiftly withers. Why? Paradoxically, looking closer at the vice of pride can help us understand the virtue of humility. Comprehending the nature of the disease illuminates the need and function of the medicine.

Satan's Special Wine

In the twelfth century, a woman named Herrad of Landsberg (d. 1195), an abbess of Hohenburg in Alsace, crafted a vivid illustration of pride. Herrad oversaw the production of a creative medieval encyclopedia that she named the *Hortus deliciarum*,

5. Jane Foulcher, *Reclaiming Humility: Four Studies in the Monastic Tradition* (Collegeville, MN: Liturgical Press, 2015), 20.

6. Quoted in *Summa virtutum de remediis anime*, ed. and trans. by Siegfried Wenzel (Athens, GA: University of Georgia Press, 1984), 76.

the garden of delights. She saw herself as a "little bee inspired by God," collecting from the flowers of Scripture, philosophy, and theology and bringing them together into a "single sweet honeycomb" for the formation of the medieval women under her charge.[7] This honeycomb of learning included magnificent illustrations meant to instruct the nuns just as much as the text did.[8]

Herrad included a sequence on the creation of the angels on the first day.[9] On the top part of the page, God creates. He sits with his hand outstretched in blessing, angels on either side of him. The panel immediately below illustrates the making of Lucifer, most glorious of the angels. The two are placed in exactly the same way on the page, God above, Lucifer below, in a visual echo. While God is barefoot and plainly dressed, Lucifer is elaborately shod and wearing an embroidered robe. He holds emblems of authority as his wonderful wings stretch across the frame of the scene encompassing the other angels. They hold a banner across him, quoting Ezekiel 28:12 (NIV): "You were the seal of perfection, / full of wisdom and perfect in beauty."

Lucifer takes the gifts of his beauty and power and wields them for greater authority. The visual echo reinforces Lucifer's mimicry of God. Lucifer persuades the lesser angels to rebel. Lucifer puts himself in God's place, usurping his authority right on the page in front of us. Lucifer *imitates* God in excess.[10] For Herrad was

---

7. *Hortus deliciarum*, 2:4, no. 2, quoted in Danielle B. Joyner, *Painting the Hortus deliciarum: Medieval Women, Wisdom, and Time* (University Park, PA: The Pennsylvania State University Press, 2016), 3.

8. Sadly, the original manuscript, taken from the abbey and housed at the Library of Strasbourg, burned alongside the library in 1870. But many of the pages had been lovingly copied, so we can still catch a glimpse of the wonder of the *Hortus deliciarum*.

9. Traditionally, medieval people postulated that when God made light, he formed the angels too.

10. Isaiah 14:12–14.

teaching her nuns not only about the creation of the world and the fall of the angels but also about pride. As Saint Augustine of Hippo writes in his *Confessions*, "pride apes sublimity" in a silly and doomed imitation of God's glory.[11] The fourteenth-century Carmelite friar Richard Lavynham (fl. 1380) writes that "pryde is not ellys but a badde desyr of hey worschyp [pride is nothing else but a bad desire of high worship]."[12] Pride is the habitual practice of centering ourselves at the heart of the universe. In the end, this centering comes always at the cost of others, in violation of the sovereignty of God and the reality of our createdness.

I, for one, am not gathering a group of rebel angels in a misguided attempt to set myself up on the throne of God (though I admit to loving flashy shoes). Neither am I a United States senator nor a tech overlord, people who strike me as tempted to "ape sublimity." What does pride look like in most people's much smaller lives? We humans almost universally have trouble acknowledging our need, our dependence, our mistakes, or our sins—in other words, our limitations—which seem to us to detract from our worth. Like Lucifer, we can't appreciate the beauties we have been given. We are consumed by what we *could* have, what we lack, and what we owe. We do not say, alongside the psalmist, that we have "no good apart from [the Lord]," that "the boundary lines have fallen for me in pleasant places" (Ps. 16:2, 6). We often want no boundary lines at all.

All people share in varying ways a natural desire for excellence. We like being good at things. We like having good things. I am deeply proud of my children. I marvel at how I ended up

11. Augustine, *Confessions*, Book II, 13.

12. Richard Lavynham, *A Litil Tretys*, ed. J. P. W. M. van Zutphen (Rome: Institutum Carmelitanum, 1956), 1.

with these glorious creatures. What is the difference between bad and good pride? Bad pride is the habit of desire for excellence in excess, teaches Saint Thomas Aquinas.[13] If I look at my children and my heart bursts with pride not because they are who they are but because they're not like someone else's children—because they are better—I am in hot water.

This excess of pride takes many forms. I take credit for things I shouldn't. *I deserve this. That's mine. I should be in charge.* My inner dialogue follows a narrative that always ends in my favor, my superiority: I might not be the best, but thank God, I am not the worst. Thank you, Lord, for making me not like *them*—whoever *them* is in the moment: murderers, or people who cut in grocery checkout lines (Luke 18:11).

Medieval writers described pride in forms we know well: arrogance, self-conceit, vainglory, presumption. A fifteenth-century book helping layfolk confess their sins, *Jacob's Well,* describes presumption very practically: looking for public admiration, to sit first, to speak most, to take credit for the work of others or simply not give others credit, judging yourself as stronger, hardier, worthier than another person. One begins to think one earned their good fortune, goodness, prosperity, even their virtues, deservedly—for their good works or as a result of their excellent governance and cleverness.[14]

These small white lies and habits of propping up the self, in the long run, build to grand narratives of self-deception. A Middle English manual for penitents describes pride with great aplomb: "It blinds a man so that he does not know himself. This

13. *ST* II-II.162.1.2r.

14. *Jacob's Well: An English Treatise on the Cleansing of Man's Conscience*, ed. Arthur Brandeis (Oxford: Horace Hart, Printer, 1900), 69.

is a right strong and special wine of the devil."[15] We tend to drunkenly take credit for our great gifts under the influence of "Satan's special wine" (a phrase that never fails to delight me). A much later teacher in the virtues, Jane Austen (d. 1817), writes, "How quick come the reasons for approving what we like!"[16] Similarly, Aquinas writes, "A man is ready to believe what he desires very much."[17] A prideful person imagines and esteems herself as greater than she is, like a drunk frat boy trying to walk in a straight line. I start to believe I made or earned these gifts all by myself, that I do not owe anything to anyone, that I am, in one of modernity's favorite buzzwords, *self-made*.

Of course, no one in creation can claim that distinction. In pride, I reject creatureliness in favor of the pleasant deception that I too am God. I am capable of anything I set my mind to, unencumbered by the debts of community and family and friendship or even by the God-given limits of my body and mind. Modern-day theologian Joan Chittister writes, "When we make ourselves God, no one in the world is safe in our presence."[18] *Nothing* is safe from us. It is for this reason that pride is often depicted in medieval literature as a roaring, devouring *lyoun*.[19] The lion's violent appetites are unslakable. Pride can instrumentalize anything for

15. *Two Middle English Translations of Friar Laurent's Somme le Roi: Critical Edition*, ed. Emmanuelle Roux (Turnhout, Belgium: Brepols, 2010), Royal Ms A.X., 4.

16. Jane Austen, *Persuasion (Edinburgh: J. Grant, 1905), 20.*

17. *ST* II-II.162.3.2r.

18. Joan D. Chittister, *The Rule of St. Benedict: Insights for the Ages* (New York: Crossroad, 1992 [repr. 1997]), 61–62.

19. See, for instance, *Jacob's Well*, 8; or the personification of elegantly robed Pride, who holds a sword and rides a lion in *The Dunois Hours*, London, British Library, Yates Thompson MS 3, f.159r, accessed March 24, 2025, https://britishlibrary.typepad.co.uk/.a/6a00d8341c464853ef019b00775c21970b-popup?_ga=2.169452001.13456553.1742848678-843098585.1742841318r.

self-aggrandizement and power, even virtues, even holiness. In pride, I take my children, my marriage, my faith, my little gifts, my luck, the things I can take absolutely no credit for, and turn them into opportunities to prove my excellence and buttress myself against the gravity of my failures and need. Because pride can do this to any good gift, it is the first vice, the root, and the last to be eradicated.

In God's grace, pride can be uprooted only in the habitual practice of confessional humility.

Worm's Meat

If pride is Satan's special wine, humility is a splash of ice-cold water in the face, or maybe one of those green smoothies that contains all your vegetables for the day. Bitterness and sweetness both linger on the tongue. One of the most popular writers of the Middle Ages, the Cistercian abbot Saint Bernard of Clairvaux (d. 1153), wrote the premier medieval definition of humility, used over and over by writers of penitential texts, one of whom was Geoffrey Chaucer (d. 1400), who "englished" it for his readers in *The Canterbury Tales:* "Humilytee, or mekenesse . . . is a vertu thurgh which a man hath verray knowleche of himself, and holdeth of himself no pris ne deyntee, as in regard of his desertes, considerynge ever his freletee."[20] In Modern English, that's "humility, or meekness . . . is a virtue through which a person has true self-knowledge, and does not hold himself too high,

20. Geoffrey Chaucer, *The Parson's Tale* in *The Riverside Chaucer*, ed. Larry D. Benson, 3rd ed. (Boston: Houghton Mifflin Company, 1987), ll. 475–76.

but regards what he justly deserves, considering ever his frailty." Humility is full, authentic, active self-knowledge that pays particular attention to our neediness. It is a greater challenge to acknowledge our failures and limitations than to recognize our strengths and victories, and this can be a profound barrier to self-knowledge. If you interviewed people on the street, a lot of them would say they would have hidden Jews in Hitler's Germany or resisted chattel slavery in the antebellum American South, if they had been there. Yet most people in those times and spaces, normal people who wanted ordinary things, did not do those things. We want to see ourselves as special, better, different. In our ordinary lives, if pride is the voice that excuses *all* my behavior as justified, humility is the smaller voice that persistently seeks to learn: Am I really justified/right/kind/loving? Does what I said/did/desired show that to be so? Humility is true self-knowledge in practice—a raw authenticity disciplined and stripped of toxic positivity and the web of half-truths we all weave around our personas.

Because of this raw quality, medieval writers often dove into the harsh, weird, and gross when trying to conceptualize humility. That fifteenth-century confessional guide I mentioned earlier, *Jacob's Well,* urges readers cultivating humility to "despise oneself" and practice holding oneself "wretchedest, vilest, unworthiest." Stop thinking of your good deeds, and "think always of your evil."[21] It also uses a profoundly unhelpful example of humility, which tells of a French bishop. This bishop meets a leper by the way who asks, "Bishop, for your humility, wipe with your tongue out of my nose the *snevyl that hangs therein* because my nose is far too sore for a linen cloth." And the good bishop does

21. *Jacob's Well,* 245.

so, "licking slowly," and lo and behold, out falls a precious stone into the bishop's mouth, sweet smelling and bright shining. Good thing, for the leper turns out to have been an angel in disguise. "See how through his humility the precious stone of grace fell into the bishop's mouth!" trumpets *Jacob's Well*.[22]

Now, excuse my French, what the hell are we supposed to do with that? This is not one random gross passage either. A famous guide for anchorites called the *Ancrene wisse*, as well as Bernard himself, calls for humans to recognize that one is nothing more than a *vas stercorum*, which means "sack of excrement" or, as John Donne (d. 1631) would later memorably translate it, "barrel of dung."[23] You're *wermys mete*, food for worms, *Jacob's Well* adds.[24] The medieval "bestseller" *The Prick of Conscience* sneers at us that we are "foul matter" come from "vile seed."[25] I imagine you may be regretting reviving the medieval garden of the virtues at this point.

This weird style of cultivating humility conflates confessional self-knowledge with squeamish dislike of natural human limitation alongside the weakness of sin, in other words, of bodies and their messiness. It usually ends up doing more harm than good. But this medieval tradition was trying, in its harshness, to shock listeners into recollection that in the pursuit of self-knowledge there is constant danger of self-deception. And the truth is that we *are* creatures of earth. Humility comes from the root word *humus*, Latin for "soil" or "earth." We are dust, and we return to

---

22. *Jacob's Well*, 247.

23. John Donne, "Sermon LXXXVIII, Preached at a Churching," *The Works of John Donne*, ed. Henry Alford, vol. IV (London: John W. Parker, 1839), 124.

24. *Jacob's Well*, 236.

25. *Richard Morris's The Prick of Conscience*, ed. Ralph Hanna and Sarah Wood (Oxford: Pub. For the Early English Text Society by Oxford University Press, 2013), ll. 409, 445.

that dust; we fade away as flowers (Eccl. 3:20; Ps. 103:15). We should not forget our kinship to earth. More crushingly, beyond the matter of digestive processes, humans often act like sacks of excrement to one another. Look no further than the annals of history or how you last handled yourself in a heated argument. How can we hold the truthful tension of our identities: ambulating barrels of dung and yet beautiful, beloved images of God? As creatures of the cathedral and the computer? Creatures of nuclear warheads and cruel office gossip?

Clad and Enclosed in God's Goodness

So it seems we have found another snare in the practice of humility, if we believe Bernard's definition. We are caught between pride and self-loathing, absurdly high self-esteem and zero self-esteem. Postmodern Western culture has collectively decided that the first is better; medieval Europeans mostly went with the latter. This is all troubling.

Every time I have taught Bernard's definition of humility as self-knowledge of our weakness and need in practice, an audience member has asked about a different, famous definition of humility: "Humility is not thinking less of yourself; it's thinking of yourself less." This quote is commonly misattributed to C. S. Lewis, but it's actually from Rick Warren's juggernaut bestseller, *A Purpose Driven Life*.[26] This misattribution is wrong but not wrongheaded, for C. S. Lewis does make a similar argument in

26. Rick Warren, *A Purpose Driven Life: What on Earth Am I Here For?* (Grand Rapids: Zondervan, 2008), 149.

Mere Christianity.[27] It's a powerful idea that people seem to prefer because it's usually brought up as a counterpoint against the more baggage-laden, bubble-busting Bernardine concept. With this framing, I suspect humility ends up, in the long run, in less endless introspection and worrying over the self. But it's impossible to begin being humble this way.

As creatures of habit, we can't simply command ourselves to think of ourselves less often. It's like the purple elephant conundrum: Once you're told not to think about purple elephants, that's all you'll be able to think about. Look at me, thinking of myself less! A deeper problem is that many Christians are convinced that they rarely think of themselves, but really they are just avoiding introspection and examination of their own motives and actions. It's not that they don't think of themselves; they don't know themselves.[28]

The only way out of prideful self-absorption is, ironically, a graced journey *through* the self, all its good and bad. Because we are embodied creatures and not limitless minds, we think, read, talk, and learn through the prisms of our private, shared, and bodily histories. Though humility is a gift of grace, I can't learn humility apart from myself and my own falls and joys. Sometimes humility will ask me to think less of myself. A Latin treatise on the virtues, from which Chaucer would later draw his inspiration for *The Parson's Tale,* describes the humble person like the moon: It gloriously illuminates the night, yet it borrows all its

---

27. If you meet a humble man, "he will not be thinking about humility: he will not be thinking about himself at all," C. S. Lewis, *Mere Christianity* (New York: Harper Collins, 2001), 128.

28. Lewis himself has described these types of personalities very well in *The Screwtape Letters* and *The Great Divorce.*

light from the sun. It has no light of its own. The more light the moon receives from the sun, the more you can see the scarred pocks of its surface. The more we practice humility, the easier it is to see our shortcomings. Yet we shine all the brighter in the increasing light.[29] The full contours of all our frailties and beauties emerge and glimmer in the moonlight as we become more honest about ourselves.

My favorite medieval writer, the contemplative author and first woman writer in English, Julian of Norwich (d. after 1416), plays with the traditional medieval harsh bodily language in humility to test a self-knowledge beyond self-hatred. She writes,

> A man goes upright, and the food of his body is enclosed within like a beautiful drawstring purse. And when the time comes to relieve himself, the bowels are opened and closed again full cleanly. . . . For he [God] has no contempt for what he has created, nor has he disdain to serve us at the most basic office that belongs naturally to our bodies. . . . For as the body is clad in cloth, and the flesh in skin, and the bones in flesh, and the heart in the torso, so are we, soul and body, clad and enclosed in the goodness of God.[30]

Rather than feeling revolted at being a creature with digestive processes, like many a medieval commentator, Julian marvels in gratitude at the goodness of God in giving us a bodily function that cleanly rids our bodies of waste. Joan Chittister insightfully defines

---

29. *Summa virtutum*, 92.

30. Julian of Norwich, *The Writings of Julian of Norwich*, ed. Nicholas Watson and Jacqueline Jenkins (University Park, PA: The Pennsylvania State University Press, 2006), 6.28–37, my translation.

humility as "a proper sense of self in a universe of wonders."[31] Even the most humiliating of our bodily functions in its efficient beauty belongs to this "universe of wonders." Our bodies, in all their messiness and individuality, are bulwarks of humility, gifts, touchstones against the world's howl that we should be more than human. A deeper humility than mere self-contempt requires a self-knowledge that welcomes creatureliness in its fullness—paradoxically, its limits. Humility learns to see how we are clad in God's gifts.

To Nakedly Know Myself

By the gift of God, we are embodied and limited. In humility, we must also learn how to look at our darker limitations, the evils of which we are capable and do perform. We can't live in the "happy cloud-land," as Bernard of Clairvaux calls it, refusing to look inside ourselves to discern our motives and self-deceptions.[32] Without this self-knowledge, we cannot live with one another, nor can we live in truth with ourselves.

Julian believed this too. And she countered both the danger of a false humility kin to despair and self-loathing and the danger of a presumptuous pride that seeks to obscure my deepest identity: a flawed and precious embodied creature held in God's grace. She urged her readers,

> And neither on one side fall over low, inclining to despair, nor on the other side to recklessness, as if we did not care, but

31. Chittister, *The Rule of St. Benedict*, 61–62.

32. Bernard of Clairvaux, *The Steps of Humility & Pride*, trans. M. Ambrose Conway OCSO (Kalamazoo, MI: Cistercian Publications, 1989), XII.40.

> nakedly know our weakness, realizing that we could not last for the twinkling of an eye except in the keeping of grace, and reverently cleave to God, in him alone trusting. . . . We accuse ourselves, willfully and truthfully seeing and knowing our falling and all the harms that come of it, seeing and understanding that we may never restore it; and immediately, that we willfully and truly see and know his everlasting love that he has for us, and his plenteous mercy. Thus, graciously to see and know both together is the humble accusing that our good Lord asks of us.[33]

"Humble accusing" is a tricky phrase. But it means nothing more than to "nakedly know our weakness." I must leave behind my self-deception and, with much flinching and painful humiliation, learn how I have hurt other people and myself.[34] Yet this knowledge is nothing without holding inseparably with it the everlasting love and mercy of God. There is never one without the other. One cannot practice self-contempt for long in this dispensation. Wonder and gratitude are the proper companions of humility. In confessional knowledge emptied of self-loathing, we leave the temptation to become self-flagellating, perfectionistic penitents. We can begin to embrace our truest, deepest identity: beloved children of God. Julian states it almost baldly: "And I understood no higher stature in this life than childhood, in feebleness and failing of strength and understanding."[35] To become humble like a child is to reject false narratives of control

33. Julian of Norwich, 52.53–68.

34. Karen Swallow Prior has a wonderful chapter on this aspect of humility in particular in the works of Flannery O'Connor, in *On Reading Well: Finding the Good Life through Great Books* (Grand Rapids: Brazos, 2018), ch. 12.

35. Julian of Norwich, 63.36–38.

and perfection, to understand myself as loved, limited, needy (Matt. 18:1–5).

On Imitating God (Again)

Graciously, shockingly, as we understand ourselves as children of God, our overreaching imitation of God is slowly replaced with good imitation. One anonymous medieval writer urges, "We must not think it below our dignity to become like little children, since Christ became a child, he who is boundless in power and wisdom."[36] Instead of the grasping imitation of Lucifer after sublimity and power, the death-longing to leave our limits behind, we imitate Christ in becoming a child.

If the labor of humility is to know myself in nakedness and grace, I return to my childhood in another sense too. I am called to see, repent of, and give thanks for all the selves I have been. I recognize the twenty-three-year-old, sixteen-year-old, eight-year-old I once was. I come to know my people's past and the person I am in the contexts of history, ethnicity, gender, institution, nation. Such a task often requires the aid of friends, family, historical texts, teachers, therapists, and pastors. You and I will be tempted to willfully or unconsciously protect ourselves against recognizing the full scale of the damage we have done or inherited, *while also holding on to* the constancy of our belovedness in all those moments of being and becoming ourselves. To paraphrase James K. A. Smith, I am myself and become myself in wholeness in a fuller realization of the

36. *Summa virtutum*, 90.

presence of God through my history and my body, "not above it or in spite of it."[37]

As Bernard of Clairvaux writes, "You will never have real mercy for the failings of another until you know and realize that you have the same failings in your soul."[38] I can have mercy on others. I can have mercy on myself. I can love them and myself without the competitive, life-draining drive of earning love. I can start to follow Jesus in, not in spite of, my limitations. Jesus,

> being in very nature God,
> did not consider equality with God something
> to be used to his own advantage;
> rather, he made himself nothing
> by taking the very nature of a servant,
> being made in human likeness.
> And being found in appearance as a man,
> he humbled himself
> by becoming obedient to death—
> even death on a cross! (Phil. 2:6–8 NIV)

Instead of imitating God upon his throne, we imitate Jesus in his servanthood and his humiliating death. We follow in footwashing, in his gentle teaching, in his embodiment as a helpless baby, in his attention and love to people, in how we suffer.

William of Saint-Thierry (d. 1148), friend of Saint Bernard and the abbot of Saint-Thierry of Mount Hor in the Cluniac

---

37. James K. A. Smith, *How to Inhabit Time: Understanding the Past, Facing the Future, Living Faithfully Now* (Grand Rapids: Brazos, 2023), 17. Smith's book on spiritual timekeeping is in its own way also a book on humility.

38. Bernard, *Steps*, 41.

order of Benedictines, writes, "The highest knowledge that a man can here and now attain consists in knowing in what way he does not know."[39] As children, we constantly rediscover ourselves as creatures operating in a world of wonder and mystery. In this discovery, there are endless new frontiers of ignorance and error. Sometimes our repetitive questions get answered, sometimes not. The need and dependence and joy of children in their discovery are wound together like a Celtic knot. Contained in the alternating fearful and feverish delight of question and desire lies the deepest trust that the parent *knows* and *wills* the good of the child. In Psalm 131 the psalmist sings of the weaned child with his mother,

> O Lord, my heart is not lifted up;
>   my eyes are not raised too high;
> I do not occupy myself with things
>   too great and too marvelous for me.
> But I have calmed and quieted my soul,
>   like a weaned child with its mother;
>   my soul is like the weaned child that is
>   with me.
>
> O Israel, hope in the Lord
>   from this time on and forevermore.

I recognize my inability to understand and perform. I know I will fail time and time again and that this failure is not a threat

39. *The Meditations of William of St-Thierry*, trans. A Religious of C.S.M.V. (New York: Harper & Brothers, 1954), 58.

to how I am loved. I welcome the peace of that acceptance. I trust, hope, and believe in the mercy of the Lord.

A couple of years ago, I was unloading the dishwasher. Behind me I could hear tiny, plastic plinks and a lot of focused baby breathing. Then, silence. I turned around in mild trepidation and saw that my one-and-a-half-year-old daughter, Constance, had arranged some plastic flowers from a play set upside down very, very carefully on our kitchen step stool. She had stepped back to gaze in intent admiration, hands behind her back, leaning in for a better view of the beauty she had wrought. And then the best part: She whispered under her breath, not to me or anyone else, "Yay."

Constance practiced true delight in her handiwork, a holy pride entirely compatible with humility. She had made something beautiful. She acknowledged it, rejoiced in its presence, in the good work of her little hands and mind. She had no expectations that it would be installed in the Guggenheim. She did not compare it to the more advanced artwork of her older brother and sister to prove its worth and beauty. The flowers are plastic, the body is fragile, and the work is holy. One of my favorite twentieth-century authors, Madeleine L'Engle, writes that becoming humble like children does not mean to be childish but to be childlike, to find again "our ability to be creators, our willingness to be open, to believe."[40] Children create without the presumption of godhood. Humility nourishes the other virtues and guards them from works righteousness in that fruitful tension between the firm belief that we are called into co-creation and sanctification

40. Madeleine L'Engle, *Walking on Water: Reflections on Faith & Art* (Wheaton, IL: Harold Shaw Publishers, 1980), 74.

and the sure and unafraid knowledge that we will fail. This is why every other virtue must be rooted in humility.

Loving My Creatureliness

Many years after Julian's writings on our childhood in Jesus, Friedrich Nietzsche would write, "What is good?—Everything that heightens the feeling of power in man, the will to power, power itself. What is bad?—Everything that is born of weakness."[41] But this is nonsense on a basic ontological level, for the strongest man in the world is weak and indebted. I am a creature of dust and the holy breath of God. Everything about me is dependent on greater goodness—the goodness of the air I breathe and the food I eat and the family into which I was born. I am no more truly autonomous than the child I once was in my mother's kitchen. This is the salt that keeps my work of co-creation from corrupting into wishful belief of my godhood or dominion or superiority.

When I forget my everlasting dependence, I strip myself of my very being. On the subject of pride, Saint Augustine of Hippo writes, "To abandon God and to exist in oneself, that is, to please oneself, is not immediately to lose all being; but it is to come nearer to nothingness."[42] Pride is only ever an invitation to nothingness, to the very thing that we fear and try to stave off with our own self-importance.

In humility, we move closer to somethingness, to the truthful and glorious heart of creatureliness. Out of humility's root, out of

---

41. Friedrich Nietzche, *The Antichrist*, trans. Walter Kaufmann, in *The Portable Nietzche* (New York: Penguin, 1954), §2.

42. Augustine, *Confessions*, II.13.

the knowledge of belovedness and limitation, flowers love of self, neighbor, creation, and God.

Practices and Prayer

Each chapter ends with Scripture, exercises, and a prayer. These are an invitation to meditate on or practice some of the central ideas about each virtue and vice. These are not necessary but truly invitational; try them if you wish.

> For by the grace given me I say to every one of you: Do not think of yourself more highly than you ought, but rather think of yourself with sober judgment, in accordance with the faith God has distributed to each of you. For just as each of us has one body with many members, and these members do not all have the same function, so in Christ we, though many, form one body, and each member belongs to all the others. We have different gifts, according to the grace given to each of us. (Rom. 12:3–6 NIV)

Practices

- Take time each day to get to know yourself better, as you would get to know a friend or spouse better. Spend time in reflective walks, or take a few minutes at the end of the day to think about how you acted, thought, and felt. Make this a habit.
- Make a regular practice of confession, either in your tradition's sacramental context or with a trusted friend.

- Do something this week that you really loved as a child. Watch a movie or read a book or play a game or make something. Remember your littleness and your belovedness.
- Read further on humility: *The Showings* of Julian of Norwich (I recommend the modern translation by Colledge and Walsh in the Classics of Western Spirituality Series), *The Great Divorce* by C. S. Lewis, *Life of the Beloved* by Henri Nouwen.

Prayer

Lord Jesus, teach me to really know myself—my gifts, my limitations, my errors—and let this knowledge transform how I understand myself, the world, and other people. Thank you for becoming like me, being with me, freeing me into myself as your image. May I imitate you in your incarnation rather than grasping falsely after your power and glory. Give me the open and humble heart of a child, eager to believe, eager to create, eager to love well. Amen.

CHAPTER 3

ENVY AND LOVE: BASILISK AND BLOSSOM

He said to him, "'You shall love the Lord your God with all your heart and with all your soul and with all your mind.' This is the greatest and first commandment. And a second is like it: 'You shall love your neighbor as yourself.'"

—MATTHEW 22:37–39

Love is that liquour sweet and most divine,
Which my God feels as bloud; but I, as wine.

—GEORGE HERBERT, "THE AGONIE"

In the imagination of late medieval and early modern artists, envy looked like a malicious old woman. In the famous Arena Chapel, Giotto (d. 1337) painted an Envy like this with a snake emerging from her mouth, hissing venomously into her eyes.[1] Another allegory of Envy at the Art Institute of Chicago stands wrinkly in a frame, glowering at youthful lovers embracing around her.[2] If she could, I think she would eat them. Both these Envies always remind me of the time my then-boyfriend now-husband was pedaling home from a college class and, to his lasting horror, saw his elderly neighbor sprint out into her front yard topless to spit furiously at someone.

Perhaps the most haunting is a later rendition carved in silver on a plaque now at the Walters Art Museum.[3] Winged, decrepit Envy chews and gnaws upon *her own heart*. The mastication of her heart tells us something of the fullness of envy. No mere synonym for jealousy, envy is ugly comparison that putrefies into maddened self-loathing and the willful destruction of love itself.

Medieval people often doodled and painted and prayed over hearts as symbols of love. At the abbey of Saint Walburg in Germany, an anonymous nun-artist created a series of devotional pictures in the late fifteenth century or early sixteenth century

---

1. Giotto di Bondone, *Envy*, detail from *The Seven Vices*, fresco, ca. 1306, Arena Chapel, Padua, accessed November 24, 2024, https://www.wikiart.org/en/giotto/envy-1306.

2. Cristofano Robetta, *Envy*, engraving, ca. 1505, Art Institute of Chicago, accessed November 24, 2024, https://www.artic.edu/artworks/4373/allegory-of-envy.

3. Peter Flötner, *Allegory of Envy*, silver box, ca. 1540, Walters Art Museum, Baltimore, accessed November 24, 2024, https://art.thewalters.org/detail/1336/allegory-of-envy/.

Peter Flötner, *Allegory of Envy*, silver plaque, ca. 1540, Walters Art Museum, Baltimore.
The Walters Art Museum/CC0

for her sisters' contemplation.[4] I will return to another of these hearts later in this chapter. For now, contemplate the first. A human heart has become a cottage, complete with stairs up to a door and a table. Inside the heart-house dwells the Trinity—and the possessor of the heart herself, the nun. Hair unbound

4. For more on the artist, her social context, and the motif of the house as a heart, see Jeffrey Hamburger, *Nuns as Artists: The Visual Culture of a Medieval Convent* (University of California Press, 1997), especially ch. 4.

The Heart as a House, devotional picture, ca. 1500, Staatsbibliothek zu Berlin, Berlin.
Public domain 1.0

in a sign of great intimacy, she snuggles up in the arms of the Godhead at a cozy table in fellowship. At the hand of God the Father, a scroll reads, "O my eternal love, be welcome unto me."[5] It is unclear whether these words come from the nun, welcoming the Godhead into herself, or from God, welcoming the nun, fully at home and at rest, at last, in her own heart.

With charming literalism, the picture depicts Ephesians 3:17–18 (DRA): "That Christ may dwell by faith in your hearts; that being rooted and founded in charity, you may be able to comprehend, with all the saints, what is the breadth, and length, and height, and depth." It also reminds me of the phrase I used as a child, that I myself could "invite Jesus into my heart." This domestic scene witnesses to the absolute audacity of believing that the Trinitarian Godhead, in unending breadth, length, height, and depth of love, dwells in one's own heart.

God is love (1 John 4:8). For many of us, this line has become nearly emptied of meaning. Hugh of Saint Victor (d. 1141), monastic theologian, slaps some sense back into our understanding: "Listen, O man, if you are still disposed to think it a small thing to have charity, listen; I tell you, God is charity. Is it a small thing to have God dwelling in oneself?"[6] This is the same creator God of the universe of whom a much later hymnwriter sings, "Immortal, invisible, God only wise / in light inaccessible hid from our eyes."[7] No, Hugh, surely it is not a small thing to

---

5. *The Heart as a House*, devotional picture, ca. fifteenth century, Handschriftenabteilung 417, Staatsbibliothek zu Berlin, Berlin, accessed December 3, 2024, https://digital.staatsbibliothek-berlin.de/werkansicht?PPN=PPN1783514531&PHYSID=PHYS_0003&DMDID=DMDLOG_0002.

6. Hugh of Saint-Victor, *The Divine Love*, trans. A Religious of C.S.M.V. (Oxford: A.R. Mowbray & Co, 1956), 20.

7. Walter C. Smith, "Immortal, Invisible, God Only Wise," public domain hymn.

have such a God dwelling in oneself! And this dwelling is not an abstraction. The indwelling of Love occurs in each person, in the times and places where we live right now, in our smallness. This is what the artist of Saint Walburg, whose name and face have been long lost to time, wanted to tell her sisters and what she still whispers to the lovers of Jesus today.

Envy, love's willful destruction, its diametric opposite, involves choking down the remains of your own heart. Love the virtue requires stretching and expanding your heart, knocking down walls, replacing the roof, throwing rubbish out, making room for the Godhead through love's imitation of the wildly creative character of the Creator. If Love itself, the Godhead, dwells in us, then Hugh urges us to get down to business and build a house expansive enough to contain it.

> Let no one make excuse, let no one say: '*I* cannot build a house for the Lord, my slender means are not sufficient to meet such great demands. Exile and pilgrim as I am, and dwelling in a country not my own, I lack even a site. This is a work for kings . . . How should *I* build a house for the Lord?' O man, why do you think like that? That is not what your Lord requires from you. He is not telling you to buy a piece of land from someone else in order to extend His courts. He wants to dwell in your heart—extend and enlarge that! . . . Enlarge your heart, therefore, so that you may be able to contain Him whom the whole world cannot contain. . . . Where you yourself fail in doing this, He will enlarge it for you.[8]

8. Hugh of Saint-Victor, *Selected Spiritual Writings*, trans. A Religious of C.S.M.V. (Harper & Row, 1962), *De Arca Noe Morali*, book IV, ch. 1, italics in the original.

In the cultivation of love and its divine, endless creativity, human hearts, which are generally unsuitable for habitation, become God's home. How does the heart stretch to house the Creator? And how can such a love defeat the corrosive power of envy?

The short answer is this: Learning to love God is inextricable from learning to actually love ourselves and our neighbors too.

My Inner Basilisk[9]

As you may recall, medieval writers loved to compare the soul to a garden, a greening and ripening place as one grows in love. But as the fourteenth-century pastoral work *The Book of Vices and Virtues* describes, into this holy verdancy slithers envy, a basilisk who seeks to "restrain" this lush abundance.[10] An enormous serpent with a crest, or a cock with a snake's tail, the basilisk kills with one glance. It is so overwhelmingly venomous that its breath scorches the earth: "No greenship can endure near him neither in grass, nor bush, nor trees."[11] The basilisk of envy desires another's holy green to crackle and stiffen in death.

In college I was stung by a stingray in the warm waters off Puerto Peñasco. As I bled in the ocean, I thought it was an ordinary cut—until I passed out amid the molten sharpness of venom creeping up my toes toward my heel. I had a similar experience years later in a disorientingly different context. Scrolling though

9. Great band name; feel free to use it.

10. From the text of BL Royal 18 A.X, *Two Middle English Translations of Friar Laurent's Somme le Roi: Critical Edition*, ed. Emmanuelle Roux (Turnhout, Belgium: Brepols, 2010), 12.

11. Royal 18 A.X, 12.

social media, I discovered that an author further along in their career than I am was publishing something that included Julian of Norwich, my favorite medieval writer whom I have studied for years. Promptly I began grousing in my spirit.

Bold of you to write on Julian as a nonmedievalist.

Stay in your lane.

I hope it sucks.

The last thought in particular twanged dissonantly, which caused me to pause. Why would I want someone else, a talented and thoughtful person I respect, to fail? Then, a scalding moment of clarity: *I am envious.* Envy initially felt like an ordinary cut, something my mind could justify. But the vicious wishes spread without check, as venom in a bloodstream, smoldering and necrotic.

Like covetousness, envy entails the desire for something one does not possess. But this desire does not stop there. John of Damascus (d. 749), the Arab monk and polymath, wrote the most enduring definition of envy, used by nearly every prominent writer of the later Middle Ages. Curiously, he describes envy as a kind of pain: "Envy is pain over the good fortune of others."[12] Along with some other medieval thinkers, Thomas Aquinas describes this pain as "sorrow."[13] The English Carmelite friar Richard Lavynham, in his little treatise on the vices, puts it like this: "Envy is the sorrow which one creature has when another

12. John of Damascus, *An Exposition of the Orthodox Faith*, trans. E. W. Watson and L. Pullan, *Nicene and Post-Nicene Fathers, Second Series*, vol. 9, ed. Philip Schaff and Henry Wace (Buffalo, NY: Christian Literature Publishing Co., 1899), revised and edited for *New Advent* by Kevin Knight, Book II, Ch. 14, accessed November 24, 2023, https://www.newadvent.org/fathers/33042.htm.

13. *ST* II-II.36.1.

fares well—or the gladness that he fares evil."[14] (Like my pathetic "I hope it sucks.") The envious person is not content simply to observe that the grass is greener on the other side; envy wishes that grass to wilt in the exhale of its poisonous breath.

This element of inward or outward sorrowing and rejoicing is the key to understanding envy. Envy extends into something personal, a sideways statement about the respective values of the envier and the envied one. Envy compares. This is also why envy feels so wretched, like a cheese grater taken to the soul. *My superiority is proven through your failure. You don't deserve that car/job/spouse/trip/recognition, but I do.* Envy distracts the envier from their own feelings of inadequacy. In other words, envy hits too close to home for us to wish to examine it, for it is wrapped up in our deepest personal discontents or insecurities about our lives. It's easier to lash out at another person than to deal with one's own feelings and fears.

I used to pretend I wasn't an envious person. The colorful fifteenth-century penitential aid *Jacob's Well* tells me I am not the only one. The anonymous author observes that envy is seldom confessed to friends or to spiritual advisors because its hold on our spirits is tight.[15] Even from ourselves, we hide envy, shrouding it in other, more reasonable, less humiliating emotions or rationales. Such cloaking is relatively easy because envy promotes stupidity or an excess amount of "false judgments," in the words of *The Book of Vices and Virtues*.[16] One begins to begrudge things that are ridiculous objects of grievance—I don't own Julian of

---

14. Richard Lavynham, *A Litil Tretys*, ed. J. P. W. M. van Zutphen (Rome: Institutum Carmelitanum, 1956), 13.

15. *Jacob's Well: An English Treatise on the Cleansing of Man's Conscience*, ed. Arthur Brandeis (Oxford: Horace Hart, Printer, 1900), 86.

16. *The Book of Vices and Virtues: A Fourteenth Century English Translation of the Somme Le Roi of Lorens d'Orleans*, ed. W. Nelson Francis (Oxford: Oxford University Press, 1998), 23.

Norwich. In envy, judgment sours and curdles like old milk. If it weren't so painful, it would be funny.

Because of our ingenuity in masking this humiliating vice, envy can be hard to identify. To counter this blindness, medieval penitential manuals have lists of envious behavior meant to act as mirrors to our hearts and minds that goad readers into recognition of our envious behavior. Envy proceeds along a well-worn human path: causing certain ways of speaking and bitterness of heart; unbinding friendships; sowing discord, scorn, accusations; putting impediments in the way of those who wish to do right; and finally, inspiring acts of malignity like property damage or public slander.

For many of us, rarely do things progress so far in our envy that we burn down the house we long for, steal the boyfriend or car we want for ourselves, or murder the person we're jealous of, though the envious do all those things. Instead, we idly wish these or lesser evils in our heart or with our lips, which is, as Jesus reminds us, still the sin (Matt. 5:22). Envy tends to surface in the way we think or talk about other people when they are not around. Medieval writers divided these modes of thinking and speaking into a marvelous triad of envious language: backbiting, grouching, and murmuration. Grouching and murmuration both sound exactly like what they are: ongoing low-level resentment of someone else's success voiced either in loud complaints to a friend (grouching) or malicious sideways whispers couched in quiet (murmuration). Chaucer's Parson explains at length the habits of the envious backbiter:

> Some man praises his neighbor but with wicked intent, for he always makes a wicked knot at last end. Always he makes a

> "but" at last end, that is worthy of more blame than is worth all the praising. The second species is that if a man be good and does or says a thing to good intent, the backbiter will turn all that goodness upside-down to his malicious intent. The third is to reduce the bounty of his neighbor. The fourth species is if men speak goodness of such a man, then will the backbiter say, "by my faith, such a man is yet better than he," in dispraising of the man that men praised. The fifth species is this: to consent gladly and harken gladly to the harm that men speak of other folk.[17]

Chaucer's list makes me laugh and cringe. The "but" we add to the end of the sentence after Trojan horse praise, the comparisons snuck into conversation, the silent pleasure in others' trash-talking—they are all too familiar. One Latin fourteenth-century preacher's handbook describes it well: "Honey in mouth and words of milk / But gall in heart and fraud in deeds."[18] And to think that neither Chaucer nor our preacher compiler had ever seen backbiting, grouching, or murmuration in their perfected form on social media!

Envy weeps when others rejoice and rejoices when others weep. In envy there is no fruit or fellowship or growth—only opposition. The primeval paradigm of envy, Cain's murder of his brother Abel, still haunts us (Gen. 4). Envy is the "mother of death."[19] In stark contrast, love is the giver of life (1 John 3:14).

---

17. Geoffrey Chaucer, *The Parson's Tale* in *The Riverside Chaucer*, ed. Larry D. Benson, 3rd ed. (Boston: Houghton Mifflin Company, 1987), ll. 493–497.

18. *Fasciculus Morum: A Fourteenth-Century Preacher's Handbook*, ed. and trans. Siegfried Wenzel (University Park, PA: The Pennsylvania State University Press, 1989), 173.

19. *Book*, 22.

The devouring and comparative self-loathing of envy is destroyed only by the creative capacities of love. Love weeps with those who weep and rejoices with those who rejoice (Rom. 12:15).

The Fourfold Bloom: Objects of Love

Our human love is the outpouring of divine, uncreated Love in which we move and live and breathe. In it, we mimic the loving act of creation itself. As a result, love is fundamentally creative and diverse. At times love chastises, love welcomes, love mourns, love rejoices, love is patient, love is kind, and so on, and so on. Each virtue is actually a form of love in disguise. So love is difficult to pin down and discuss in the same manner as, say, fortitude or patience. A more helpful and practical way to think about love is by its object.

In medieval writing of the vices and virtues, one of the most popular representations of the human practice of love was a four-petaled plant that some scholars argue is a flower, others the four-leaf clover often tied to luck today. Each petal or leaf represented a created love aimed toward a different recipient. This flower was named the *quatrefoil* or *quadrifoil*, or in Middle English, a *trewe-love*. The preacher's handbook *Fasciculus morum* describes each petal of the bloom of charity in a little rhyme:

> Love God most, over any other thing
> And yourself, without overreaching,
> And your friend, through nature's teaching,
> And your foe, vengeance rejecting.[20]

20. *Fasciculus morum*, 198. Translation mine.

God-love, self-love, neighbor-love, enemy-love. The latter three loves are held together in power by the first. Each petal opens up a facet in the practice of love that enlarges the heart as the home of God.

Love of God

First, God-love. Saint Thomas Aquinas writes that the love between God and ourselves is more like friendship than other kinds of human love, such as vassal to lord, parent to child, or lover to lover.[21] The poet of the Middle English *Pearl* describes the character of God and the quality of God's relationship to him after an account of intense personal grief: "I have found Him both day and night / A God, a Lord, *a frende* full fine."[22] The line successively telescopes our distance from the Creator: from cosmic God, to authoritative lord, to good friend in our need. Perhaps this description of friendship between Creator and human feels surprising. What does friendship with God look like?

On the most fundamental level, friends share life and all its joys, hopes, worries, and interests together. This shared life together is characterized by enthusiastic and ongoing choice: Unlike with my children, siblings, or parents, I fully choose my friends. This, too, is true of God. God does not love us despite himself or against his better judgment but fully chooses us with delight, in creation, in crucifixion, in resurrection, in eternal life. Friendship also necessitates communication—in the case of our human-divine friendship, prayer. The habit of prayer is a chief way of loving God as truest friend. In friendship, even the most

21. *ST* II-II.23.1.

22. "Pearl," *The Poems of the Pearl Manuscript*, ed. Malcolm Andrew and Ronald Waldron (University of Exeter Press, 2007 [repr. 2010]), ll. 1203–1204.

different friends tend to become more like each other over the years. And in prayer and the sacraments, that is exactly what happens. Christ has already drawn near to us. Then we, gradually and through these practices, awaken to our preexisting closeness to him and become more like him.

Even the most dedicated practice of friendship can only fully be described as a gift. Think of your dearest friends. When you met them, could you have foreseen how they would shape your life and person as they have? How they would willingly join you in the dark places, rejoice with you in the light, overcome conflict with you? These human friendships are like small windows into the greater glorious light of unearned friendship with God.

Love of Self

Love of God inherently sloshes over like a fountain into love of self, the next petal of the medieval quadrifoil. In one way, self-love is a natural love tied closely to the self's sheer created existence. The Lord looked at you when he created you and said in complete simplicity, "This is good." Things have gone terribly awry, humans instinctively recognize, when we starve and torture our bodies and lie to our minds and hearts. We are made to value and protect our bodies, our special interests, the delightfully unique way each of us interacts with and loves creation.

It is simple in another way. Every night, in her usual attempts to forestall bedtime, my three-year-old daughter gravely proclaims to me in the manner of a benediction, "Jesus woves you." Usually she waits a beat, then adds expectantly, "Did you needed to hear dat?" I always answer in equal solemnity, "Yes, I did." Imagine a friend introducing you to someone else: "This is [insert your name], *God's dear friend.*" I sit up a little straighter, my constricted

Grinch-heart suddenly feeling a bit more capacious. Though envy might be mistakenly characterized as excessive self-love, it truly stems from deficient self-love: a corset-tight understanding of the self as valuable only in the light of her own successes, skills, virtues, beauties, and independence. These are good things, but they're not the origin of any human's value. Self-love grounded in achievement is easily threatened by the successes, gifts, and beauties of other people. The insecure, envious self has forgotten she is a friend of God, loved by God dearly, *as she is* (Rom. 5:8). Nothing material is capable of confirming her intrinsic worth outside of her bare beloved existence. True self-love entails welcoming oneself as a dear friend of God. And just as with interpersonal friendships, befriending myself will not happen in defensiveness nor deception nor combativeness nor cruelty. Real self-love brims with grace and unvarnished honesty.

If I am of incalculable, inherent worth by virtue of my created existence and God's love for me, then the logic proceeds inexorably. My neighbor and my enemy possess the same worth as I do because such worth is never dependent on what I have done or failed to do. God-love and true self-love insistently bubble over into love of neighbor.

Love of Neighbor

On to the third petal of the quadrifoil: Christ commands us to love our neighbors as ourselves (Mark 12:31). The overflow of God-love and self-love into neighbor-love partially comes from the inherent mechanics of the sacraments, particularly the Eucharist and baptism. These sacraments not only signify God's work in the world but actually work unity. In the body of Christ, his church, the penitential manual *Jacob's Well* reminds us that we are

> christened in one baptism, bought by one price, one money, which is Christ's blood. . . . We have all one truth & we be bound by one law. . . . We all have one lord, that holdeth us, body & soul, under his shield. . . . We are all fellows in God's host, that each day fight as his knights, and all we abide in one garrison. . . . We are all of one spirit to live spiritually as we live here bodily. Through that spirit we are chosen God's children.[23]

The anonymous author ends with this Pauline exhortation: "We are all limbs of one body. The body is holy church, the head is Christ & we are the limbs."[24] The metaphor reminds us what it means to love our neighbors as ourselves—because in at least one very real sense, our neighbors *are* ourselves.

If we are truly in Christ's body together, this natural bodily care and mutuality changes how we relate to one another in action and thought. *The Book of Vices and Virtues,* which shares the same source as *Jacob's Well,* lovingly expands this idea: In the body, "when a foot stumbles or slides, the other helps it immediately; when someone tries to smite the head, the hand intervenes and takes the blow instead."[25] When a person is healthy, such actions are reflexive and natural. When part of the body is sick, the other members work hard to compensate, to promote healing. If one eye is blind, the other eye sees for it. If a leg is broken, the muscles of the body keep it off the ground to let it heal. Cutting off limbs is a last resort.

Such an idea does not mean, of course, that only Christians are our neighbors. God beckons this body of love to move out

23. *Jacob's Well,* 253–4.
24. *Jacob's Well,* 254.
25. *Book,* 147.

into the needy world that does not know Christ. Saint Augustine of Hippo preached on 1 John to a group of freshly baptized new Christians:

> *God is love.* What sort of countenance does love have? What sort of shape does it have? What sort of height does it have? What sort of feet does it have? . . . No one can say. Yet it has feet, for they lead to the Church. It has hands, for they stretch out to the poor person. It has eyes, for that is how he who is in need is understood: *Blessed,* it says, *is he who understands concerning the needy and the poor* (Ps 41:1). It has ears, of which the Lord says, *He who has ears to hear, let him hear* (Lk 8:8). These aren't distinct members occupying space but he who has charity sees everything all at once with his understanding. Dwell there, and you shall be indwelled. Abide there, and you shall be abided in."[26]

We can tell from the manuscript recording Augustine's words that at this point, the church was roaring with enthusiasm, amen-ing up to the rafters. Augustine calms them down, saying, if you like it so much, practice it! Love already lives in you; follow the invitation to dwell in the house of Love with your actions.

Love of Enemy

With that exhortation, we reach the most unattractive petal of the quadrifoil. "Also in the name of neighbor is comprehended your enemy," reminds Chaucer's Parson to his fellow pilgrims on

26. Saint Augustine of Hippo, "Seventh Homily," *Homilies on the First Epistle of John*, trans. Boniface Ramsey (New City Press, 2008), 111–12.

the road to Canterbury. He continues, "[O]ur enemies have more need of love than our friends . . . in that same deed [love of enemy] have we remembrance of the love of Jesus Christ that died for his enemies. . . . For right as the devil is discomfited by humility, right so is he wounded to the death by love of our enemy."[27]

Loving an enemy, the Parson reminds us, most closely imitates Jesus on the cross. Enemy-love is also Christ's most radical and difficult commandment. How do I love someone who is doing bad things or hurting me or is a person I simply do not like?

One primary way Christians have expressed love for their enemies has been through correction and chastisement in the name of reform or discipline. Correction is a legitimate and necessary practice of love. Martin Luther King Jr. wrote a masterclass of enemy-love in the "Letter from Birmingham Jail." Those who call out cover-ups and abuse in the church today practice a prophetic and grueling enemy-love.

But correction and exhortation aren't the only forms of enemy-love, though they are powerfully important. There are dangers in limiting love of enemies to chastisement or correction. Too frequently we practice hubris in mistaking our own judgment and disdain for love. Many would-be reformers on social media are only too willing to cry *heretic* or threaten violence in the name of "loving" their enemies. Such correction rarely emerges from love, but more often from self-aggrandizement, fear of a perceived threat, anger, or envy itself. Without the constant work of humility and discernment, every follower of Christ is in danger of this trap. The Middle Ages is a depressing mirror for us in this regard. For every impassioned exhortation to enemy-love, there

27. Chaucer, *The Parson's Tale*, ll. 527–29.

are anti-Semitic miracle tales calling for the murder of the Jews or for crusade on Muslims, as medieval Christians considered both people groups as enemies. Damningly, often these calls to enemy-love and "corrective" tales coexist in the same pages. The *Canterbury Tales* features both the love-preaching Parson *and* the bloodthirsty anti-Semitic tale of the Prioress.[28] This is one among too many examples to list. But we should be wary of thinking ourselves in modernity more capable of controlling our contempt for the people we think are our enemies.

There are no silver bullets that solve the problem of loving our enemies, beyond recognizing that Christ himself did. The call to enemy-love shatters all latent Pelagianism, all hopeful pretenses that I can become truly loving on my own, do this human wholeness gig all by myself. Like a true American, I want to believe the creed that I can do it if I just set my mind to it. I simply need to practice! Really will it, *more firmly* this time. But I am always sobered up by spending time in the company of people I do not like—or seeing them on a screen or hearing their voice. Enemy-love is a practice in which I continually fail.

Yet I sense the unity of the quadrifoil at work: Paying attention to my failures to love my enemies leads me back into God-love, into the heart of prayer. God, you will have to love my enemies for me, and somehow then I can become more like you. And strangely, according to the great Saint John Chrysostom, enemy-love through prayer also leaks back into self-love: "When

28. Sometimes critics argue that the Prioress's tale is satirical. But the tale closely aligns with a very popular genre of antisemitic contemporary miracle tales and is too close to the original to comfortably be read as satire (and indeed for much of its existence was read straightforwardly regardless of authorial intention). I hope, for Chaucer's sake, that it is satirical, but I doubt it.

we pray for our enemies, we commend not so much them as ourselves to God, and we are heard more when we pray for our enemies than when we pray for ourselves. He who prays for himself performs not an act of grace but of nature; but he who prays for his enemy performs an act of grace."[29]

In the graced act of praying for our enemies, in loving brothers and sisters and selves, we pass from death into life (1 John 3:14). Even if such prayer is given from a distance with much gritting of teeth.

Safe in the Heart of Jesus

How could any of us wounded and wounding creatures love like Jesus loves? It is impossible for me to love like that. I know this about myself. Yet in the grace of God, beyond belief, this stumbling block is the juncture of humility and love that becomes the beating heart of the Christian. If love involves weeping with those who weep, rejoicing with those who rejoice, and all the variations of that formula, love fundamentally practices *withness*. Emmanuel, God with us, is the beginning, middle, and end of love. Only in the grace of Christ's life, teaching, death, and resurrection, in what he has already given, in his presence, in the fullness of his *being with us* deeper than we are ever fully aware, does this radical life of love become possible.

The art of the anonymous artist of Saint Walburg vividly shows us, again, the reality of this life of love. In another devotional piece, the nun has drawn the conventional subject of Jesus

29. As quoted in the *Summa virtutum*, 112.

Christ on the cross, the ultimate medieval image of love. Yet unconventionally, where his torso would normally be, she has drawn a giant heart. Inside that heart dwells the infant Christ, holding something like a pyx, and a habited nun.[30]

30. *The Heart on the Cross,* devotional picture, ca. 1500, Saint Walburg, Eichstätt; found in Hamburger, *Nuns as Artists,* plate 10. This is another variation of the side wound imagery that I discuss more in *Jesus through Medieval Eyes.*

Christ's Heart on the Cross, devotional picture, ca. 1500, Saint Walburg, Eichstätt.
Jeffrey F. Hamburger

Our artist, as good medieval artists often do, blatantly disregards time and space. How can baby Jesus be present in the heart of dying Jesus? With a host? We no longer inhabit a time-bound narrative that proceeds chronologically. Instead, we are in the time of contemplation, or of *kairos*, the fullness of time, which rips the thin veils of time and place to show us where we stand. As is common in devotional art, the nun is meant to be a placeholder for the viewer, for us. She shows us a reality beyond what we can easily see. In Christ's grace, we are given Christ, dwell in the heart of Christ, alongside Christ. The excess is both weirdly, perfectly medieval and perfectly in line with the superabundance of God. It expresses the same idea as the all-encompassing "I am" proclamations of Christ in the gospel of John: I am the bread, I am the light, I am the door, I am the good shepherd, I am the resurrection, I am the way and the truth and the life, I am the vine. "I it am, I it am . . . I it am that thou longest," Christ tells Julian of Norwich.[31] It is the invitation of John 15:4: "Abide in me as I abide in you." We already dwell in the heart of God because he has loved us and died for us even in our hatreds and profound lack of love (Rom. 5:8–9). Amid our unceasing need and relentless failures, we are comforted that the crucifixion and resurrection witness to restoration as taking place in a real wound inflicted by real people.

Only by clinging to this preexisting reality can we enlarge our hearts and love one another in the fullness of the love of Jesus. Your beloved is already loved; your enemy is already loved. You are already loved.

---

31. Julian of Norwich, *A Revelation of Love,* 26.4–6.

A Flowing Reformation of Desire

The medieval mystical writers are strangely attached to the idea of divine love as *flowing*. The Trinity is a fountain overflowing with love, soaking creation with the water of life.[32] Blood flows from Christ's wounds, washing the broken, filling to the chalice brim and then the entire universe.[33] Light flows into darkened places, bringing the unseen to recognition, dispelling fear, dispensing justice.[34] What is left for us to do but ask in all seriousness for the kind of flowing love that changes hearts, carving the contours of our desire as the Colorado River carved out the Grand Canyon from stone? I do not particularly want to love my enemy. I sometimes do not even want to love my husband. I often do not want to love myself. The glorious good news is that we're not required to will ourselves into love, but like children asking a loving parent for bread, we assuredly will receive what we ask for when we ask to "learn to love . . . and leave all else."[35] We will not love well unless we want to love well—unless we undergo a reformation of our desires.

This reformation of desire will require that we let go of comparison and futile scraping for superiority. It will ask that I lean into the reality that I am already loved in my limitations, and so is my neighbor, and so is my enemy. The all-encompassing love leaves no room for envy's sad self-destruction. But how can one even begin, when active, flowing love like this feels so daunting?

---

32. Mechthild of Hackeborn, *The Book of Special Grace*, trans. Barbara Newman (New York: Paulist, 2017), 93.

33. Julian of Norwich, *A Revelation of Love*, chapter 12.

34. A favorite idea of Mechthild of Magdeburg, *The Flowing Light of the Godhead*, trans. Frank Tobin (New York: Paulist, 1998).

35. William Langland, *Piers Plowman* B-text, XX.208.

The twelfth-century monk William of Saint-Thierry boldly claimed friendship with God despite his own shortcomings. In his beautiful collection of essays on the love of God, *Meditations*, William acknowledges his lack of love—and his desire: "If, then, Thou askest me to-day, 'Lovest thou Me?' as once Thou askedst the blessed apostle, I hesitate to answer, 'Thou knowest that I love Thee,' but I do readily and with clear conscience make reply, 'Thou knowest that I *want* to love Thee.'"[36]

And William then prays for his own will: God, give me a "great will," an "enlightened" will, a "will upon which love has laid its hand."[37]

One's love may not exist yet. But, in sheer grace, all this far-fetched charity begins in simple longing. Lord, you know I want to love you. If God-love or neighbor-love or self-love, let alone enemy-love, feel impossible, keep asking and listening and looking. "Ask God that you may love one another," Saint Augustine urges.[38] Christ will not let such a prayer go unanswered, for he has commanded it. But I gather from looking at the lives of holy folks and Christ himself that your prayer to learn to love will almost certainly be answered in ways unexpected and strange.

Practices and Prayer

> Abide in me as I abide in you. Just as the branch cannot bear fruit by itself unless it abides in the vine, neither

36. William of Saint-Thierry, *Meditations*, trans. A Religious of C.S.M.V. (New York: Harper & Brothers, 1954), 90–1.

37. Saint-Thierry, *Meditations*, 91.

38. Saint Augustine, "Tenth Homily," *First John*, 154.

can you unless you abide in me. I am the vine; you are the branches. Those who abide in me and I in them bear much fruit, because apart from me you can do nothing. Whoever does not abide in me is thrown away like a branch and withers; such branches are gathered, thrown into the fire, and burned. If you abide in me and my words abide in you, ask for whatever you wish, and it will be done for you. My Father is glorified by this, that you bear much fruit and become my disciples. As the Father has loved me, so I have loved you; abide in my love. If you keep my commandments, you will abide in my love, just as I have kept my Father's commandments and abide in his love. I have said these things to you so that my joy may be in you and that your joy may be complete. (John 15:4–11)

Practices

- Read the entirety of the First Epistle of John in a different translation or a different language than you normally read (BibleGateway.com has many translations you can use for free). Sit with it.
- Reflect on these questions with a trusted friend, family member, or spouse:
  - *What do I think John means when he writes "God is love"?*
  - *Whom do I have trouble loving in the medieval quadrifoil?*
- Every day this week, pray for discernment on invitations to love from the medieval quadrifoil: Lord, how can I love my neighbor? How can I love you? How can I love myself? How can I love my enemy? See what comes out of deliberate prayer. Act on it.

- Read further on love: Saint Augustine of Hippo's *Homilies on the First Epistle of John*, *The Love That Is God* by Frederick Bauerschmidt, *The Dean's Watch* by Elizabeth Goudge.

Prayer

Lord Jesus, thank you for being Love itself. Free my will and all its desires into loving well. Help me to love you. Help me to love my neighbor. Help me to love my enemy. Help me to love myself. Transform my heart into your home; open my eyes to my eternal and safe home in you. Only in this knowledge can I flow in and with and through your love. Make me a conduit of your love for the whole world. Show me how, right now, and give me the courage and attention to listen and see and act in that love. Amen.

CHAPTER FOUR

WRATH AND MEEKNESS: SWORD AND PILLOW

Blessed are the meek, for they will inherit the earth.

—Matthew 5:5

The meek shall inherit the earth—but not its mineral rights.

—attributed to J. Paul Getty

If there is anybody in this land who thoroughly believes that the meek shall inherit the earth, they have not often let their presence be known.

—attributed to W. E. B. Du Bois

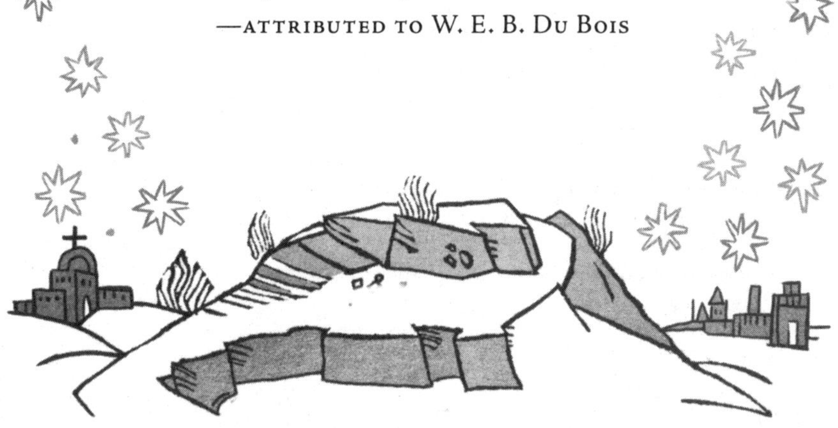

Imagine a medieval play put on in the town square. A makeshift castle stands. Around it, various personifications of virtues and vices are wildly waging war upon one another to win this castle, which one begins to realize is the soul of a person in temptation.[1] In what reads as *The Screwtape Letters* meets weird slapstick comedy, a Bad Angel leads the assault, sending out the three spiritual vices of Pride, Envy, and Wrath. They are inexplicably beaten back when the virtues of Humility, Charity, and Patience pelt them, not with sharp objects or even rotten tomatoes but with *roses*. Wrath bewails his fate:

> I, Wrath, now sing "Wail-a-woe."
> Patience gave me a painful blow.
> I am all beaten black and blue,
> With a rose that from the Cross was torn. [2]

The Bad Angel is disgusted at the vices' total lack of efficacy against the virtues. In a line that I can only imagine as a hit performed live, he shrieks at them, "Get out of here, you are not worth a turd!"[3] That phrase really is in the Middle English; I did not make it up.

---

1. The allegory of the virtues and vices in battle is a very long tradition, going back to Prudentius's Psychomachia (ca. early fifth century AD).

2. I, Wrethe, may syngyn "Weleawo. / Pacyens me gaf a sory dynt. / I am al betyn blak and blo / Wyth a rose that on Rode was rent." *The Castle of Perseverance*, ed. David N. Klausner (Kalamazoo, MI: Medieval Institute Publications, 2010), ll. 2217–2220. Translation mine.

3. "Go hens, ye do not worthe a tord." *Castle*, l. 2226.

In the strangeness of the allegory of *The Castle of Perseverance,* I can see my discomfort with this set of virtues reflected back to me. There's an otherworldly unbelievability, even absurdity, in the belief that patience will, in the end, overcome the violence of wrath. How can a rose beat Fury itself black and blue? Let's throw roses from the Cross at them; let's extravagantly strew beauty born of suffering in the face of cruelty. How? Why?

Patience is hard enough; meekness, a medieval subcategory of patience, is worse.[4] Medieval thinkers wrote that patience governs our response to suffering under external hardship, from traffic to the devastation of bodily illness and loss. Meekness is the type of patience that measures our anger in particular (as opposed to, say, sadness or disengagement in challenges). But let's be honest: If you put all the remedy virtues in a hat and then pulled one out, would there be a more disappointing virtue to get than meekness? Chastity certainly gets a lot of people down, but meekness in particular has the flavor of defeat, of the kind of "virtue" that the powerful smilingly impose upon the powerless. *Bear your trials meekly,* the slaveowner lectures the enslaved man. *Authority is my burden to bear, and meekness is yours,* the husband instructs the wife. *Submit with meekness to my authority, however imperfect it may be,* condescends the lord to the peasant.

Power relations aside, many people in modernity treat meekness as a vice rather than a virtue, similar to timidity or mealy-mouthed cowardice. When I googled meekness, the example sentence provided was, no joke, "All his best friends make fun of

4. See, for instance, *ST* II-II.136.2.2r.

him for his meekness."[5] Many Christians outright reject meekness too—think of the spitting rage displayed online by so many who profess to follow Christ.

But Christ himself blesses and commends meekness; Christ himself is a model of meekness and patience. Jesus says, "Blessed are the meek, for they will inherit the earth" (Matt. 5:5) and urges us to follow him. Because he is "meek and lowly in heart" (Matt. 11:29 KJV), he can't be recommending something tantamount to cowardice, or a timid refusal to engage, or feminine reticence, or the forced submission of those who have been abused under the powerful. What could all this mean? Before we can answer that, we have to think about anger. Meekness, patience, and the vice they counteract, wrath, all confusingly hover around habits of anger.

The Fire That Nourishes, the Fire That Kills

Now we turn to another mise-en-scène, this time one of inevitable trouble: 1229, the holiday now known as Mardi Gras, a bar by the famed University of Paris, teenage boys away from home.[6] A group of students drank too much, then violently argued with the tavern owner over the bill. Beginning Lent with a bang, the rancorous boys returned on Ash Wednesday, enthusiastically rioted, and trashed the surroundings. The queen sent city guardsmen to get the area under control, and the guardsmen killed some students indiscriminately in vengeance.

5. Google Search, "Meekness," accessed August 27, 2023.

6. In those days, boys started attending university as young as twelve or thirteen. No girls, of course.

In outrage, the entire university promptly went on strike. Students traveled elsewhere, to Oxford or Toulouse, masters dispersed, and Paris's economy suffered as the Latin Quarter, the home of the university, emptied out for *two years*. When the pope and the French crown finally reached an agreement so the university could reopen, the shape of the university had been permanently changed—the strike was a powerful weapon against state violence directed toward students and issues like rent-gouging by greedy landlords.[7]

This violent episode illustrates the complexity of anger: spur-of-the-moment arguments, chaotic mob rage, revenge, murder—and the organized righteous anger that often drives social change. Anger has lit the fuse of some of the most awful behavior in history, from the deadly mob rage of January 6, 2021, down to the elderly man I saw in the city pool, begoggled face mottled red and pink, bellowing, "You son of a . . ." at his lane partner when they lightly bumped arms. Yet anger can and has also fueled some of the greatest movements in history, from public sanitation to workers' rights.

Wrath is not synonymous with anger; meekness and patience are not synonymous with avoidance of anger. In his brick of a tome, *City of God*, Saint Augustine of Hippo categorizes anger as a passion.[8] He did not mean a passion in our more modern sense, like a beloved hobby, but a reactive stirring in our bodies and souls. In contrast to the Stoic philosophers, who believed that any movement of the passions was wrong and lessened a person's

---

7. See the account of Matthew of Paris, in Frederick Duncalf and August Krey, *Parallel Source Problems in Medieval History* (New York: Harper Brothers, 1912), 145–50, accessed August 15, 2023, https://archive.org/details/parallelsourcepr00dunciala/page/150/mode/2up.

8. Saint Augustine, *City of God*, trans. Henry Bettenson (Penguin, 2003), 14.6.

ability to make good moral decisions, Augustine argued that the main human passions, like sorrow, anger, pleasure, and fear, are value neutral. The virtuousness or viciousness of the passion in question depends on how the passion is handled, where it is directed, and its level of intensity.

Modern-day ethicist Zac Cogley explains it clearly in a threefold scheme: Anger can be virtuous or vicious by how well it evaluates wrongdoing, how it motivates the angry person, and how that anger is communicated.[9] Anger cannot be virtuous if it fails any one of those points. If you're angry for a great reason but communicate recklessly or with intent to harm, or if you have good communication but are insufficiently or overly angry, or if your anger is impeccably handled but for a bad reason, it is wrathful. Virtuous anger is connected not to a mindless response but to good judgment and even mercy. Pope Gregory the Great wrote, "Reason opposes evil all the more effectively when anger ministers at her side."[10]

Anger was part of what medieval writers like Saint Thomas Aquinas called the "irascible" power of the soul, meaning our ability to overcome resistance and defend things that need defending.[11] To simplify, our anger helps us to "gird our loins," to overcome our natural human aversion to difficult or unpleasant things and fight obstacles. The great midcentury philosopher Josef Pieper calls anger "the power of resistance in the soul."[12] For Christians, anger is not to be ignored or over-

---

9. Zac Cogley, "A Study of Virtuous and Vicious Anger," *Virtues and Their Vices*, ed. Kevin Timpe and Craig A. Boyd (Oxford: Oxford University Press, 2014), 199–224.

10. Gregory, *Moralia in Job* 5:45, in Josef Pieper, *The Four Cardinal Virtues* (Notre Dame: Notre Dame University Press, 2014), 194.

11. See Aquinas, *ST* II-II.158.1; 158.2.

12. Pieper, *Four Cardinal Virtues*, 193.

spiritualized, but noticed, handled with great care, formed by our contexts, and then combatted or acted upon as the occasion calls. Augustine, Aquinas, and other theologians recognized that as embodied creatures with hormones and fight-or-flight responses (though of course they would not have used those names), living together and learning to love in our messiness in community, we would have a lot of opportunities to be angry. Some anger is an appropriate response to wickedness caused by injustice within our communities. For instance, there is something terribly wrong with a human insufficiently angry about child abuse, or a wrongful conviction of an innocent person, or church cover-ups.

William of Auvergne (d. 1249), bishop of Paris at the time of the riots, penned a fascinating book called *On Morals.*[13] Besides being bishop, William was a theologian-philosopher of the University of Paris, one of the first people in the Latin West to seriously read the new translations of Greek thinkers, like Aristotle, emerging from Muslim philosophers. In each chapter of *On Morals*, a different virtue speaks for itself, explaining its significance in the life of holiness, in the sort of earnest and occasionally, enthusiastically unhinged manner of a high school kid running for student body president.

One of the virtues we meet is Zeal, which is akin to a virtue of directing one's anger righteously and lovingly. Zeal is a guardian of the goodness of creation. One of the most helpful and ancient

13. He apparently did not handle the crisis well. Pope Gregory IX, himself a distinguished alumnus of the university, sent a scathing letter to William regretting his personal choice to make William bishop: "With what great shame do you think we are covered when some people can mock us and say: See this man you have set over the church of Paris." William of Auvergne, *On Morals*, trans. and ed. Ronald J. Teske (Toronto: Pontifical Institute of Mediaeval Studies, 2013), x.

ways to get to the bottom of anger is to ask a question of what it is protecting. Modern-day philosopher of virtue ethics Rebecca Konyndyk DeYoung notes how the ancient desert father Evagrius impels us to ask, "What is your anger guarding?"[14] William's Zeal proclaims, "I am the fire with which *the just will glow* and have already glowed *like sparks running through the reeds* (Wis. 3:7) of this world."[15] If benevolent love is like the oven, slowly warming up food without burning so that it can feed the world, zeal is more like the grill, writes William, cooking with burning and open flames.[16] (Also, weird but true to think of medieval people grilling.) Zeal is painful but purgative as it feeds and protects life together.

Fire truly is the aptest metaphor for anger in its different virtuous and vicious forms. It nourishes life, it kills germs, it seals wounds, it impels action as zeal. But anger also scalds the innocent bystander, burns the house down, or smolders in the soul, turning relationships to bitter ashes. Just as you watch a child carefully around a campfire, just as you use tongs while grilling instead of your bare hands, even good anger is not to be tossed around or cultivated lightly. We do need to feel our feelings. To shove anger down and ignore it is to miss many important signs about who you are in the world, what is just and unjust, and what you need. But turning to anger without thought time after time creates its own habits. It is the destructive, habitual blaze we turn to now—the capital vice of wrath.

---

14. Rebecca Konyndyk DeYoung, *Glittering Vices: A New Look at the Seven Deadly Sins and Their Remedies*, 2nd ed. (Grand Rapids: Brazos, 2020), 142.

15. William of Auvergne, *Morals*, 103, italics in the original.

16. William of Auvergne, *Morals*, 93.

A Bloody, Naked Sword

In the late Middle English poem *The Assembly of Gods,* Wrath rides astride a wild boar, bearing a "blody, nakyd sword."[17] The unsheathed blade reminds us of the perpetual readiness for violence that characterizes the vice of wrath, from the squabbles between my two eldest children over who gets to sit in the "first chair," to the death-dealing fury of tyrants like Vladimir Putin that blooms in war. Geoffrey Chaucer, in his *Parson's Tale,* paraphrases Aristotle on the nature of bad anger: "Wrath is a wicked will to be avenged in word or deed."[18] Chaucer divides bad anger into two varieties: sudden or hasty ire, without the advice and consent of reason, and ire to which reason fully consents.

The first is the kind of wrath that leads to voluntary manslaughter, to road rage, or to cussing out. In his characteristic dark humor, the late medieval Dutch painter Hieronymus Bosch (d. 1516) illustrates this kind of wrath on his *Table of the Seven Deadly Sins* now at the Museo del Prado in Madrid. The panel of *ira* depicts male peasants fighting as a woman attempts to separate them—or perhaps join the fracas herself.[19] One of the peasants ludicrously has an end table over his head; the other man bears a pitcher and a sword, picking up any weapon possible to get to his enemy despite the woman in his way. Something that

17. *The Assembly of Gods: Le Assemble de Dyeus, or Banquet of Gods and Goddesses, with the Discourse of Reason and Sensuality,* ed. Jane Chance (Kalamazoo, MI: Medieval Institute Publications, 1999), ll. 624–625.

18. Geoffrey Chaucer, *The Parson's Tale* in *The Riverside Chaucer,* ed. Larry D. Benson, 3rd ed. (Boston: Houghton Mifflin Company, 1987), l. 534.

19. Hieronymus Bosch, "Wrath" (detail), *Tabletop of Vices,* oil on wood, 1505–1510, Museo del Prado, Madrid.

looks like a bowler hat lies abandoned in the grass. It would be funny if it weren't deadly serious.

Hieronymus Bosch, "*Ira*," detail from *Table of the Seven Deadly Sins*, oil on wood, ca. 1505–1510, Museo del Prado, Madrid.
Artefact / Alamy Stock Photo

The brawl happens in front of a thatch-roofed cottage—the kind of bucolic place you'd expect to see in a travel ad for medieval Europe. Instead, it is transformed into a grotesque setting for intimate violence. Indeed, domestic violence is the example par excellence of this kind of wrath. It destroys the people closest to you, the ones most likely to receive the result of one's trigger-happy disposition, whether blows or sharp words. For though this wrath looks like the result of a moment, the "hastiness" Chaucer describes is a habit: a way of being in the world governed by the readiness to be offended and a disposition toward force in word or deed.

The second kind of anger, the slow-burning kind planned and reasoned out, might be called the first-degree-murder wrath. It also concerns the premeditated curse, the mean-tempered criticism, the constant irritation, the carefully crafted, devastating slight. "Chiding and reproach" can create cruel, gaping wounds in the heart. These are spiritual slaughter, taking seriously Jesus's words about murder in the heart (Matt. 5:21–22). Hate also belongs to this category. Hatred, says Chaucer, is nothing more than old wrath.[20] I imagine a formerly hot soup with a congealed layer on top of it. In hatred we gag down a meal of lumpy, cold wrath.

The effects of our wrath are partially governed by our circumstances. For peasants, it was brawls and domestic violence, for lords and princes of the church, war itself. The medieval pastoral work *The Book of Vices and Virtues* notes the especially deadly combination of wrath and power: When two lords go to war, many of the dead in the aftermath have no guilt; churches are robbed and broken; towns burned down; men, women, and children are disinherited. Anger's divisive power is never more visible than in war. The angry person is at war with another person but also, and perhaps more devastatingly, at war with himself: "When wrath is so full in a man, he torments his soul and his body so that he has no sleep or rest."[21] Or as Chaucer says, "It robs him of the quiet of his heart and subverts his soul."[22] Who hasn't argued with a spouse or friend late in the day and then seethed under the covers, unable to sleep or be at peace? *The Book* also tells us that you can tell an angry man by the way he treats those he considers beneath him: service workers, his children, the poor.

---

20. Chaucer, *Parson*, l. 561.

21. *The Book of Vices and Virtues: A Fourteenth Century English Translation of the Somme Le Roi of Lorens d'Orleans*, ed. W. Nelson Francis (Oxford: Oxford University Press, 1998), 25.

22. Chaucer, *Parson*, l. 560.

In *The Bedford Hours,* a magnificent book of prayers now found in the British Library, Wrath (*Ira*), his face horribly slack, tongue hanging out almost like a dog, plunges a knife into his own thigh in an act of nihilistic rage against the world.[23] Wrath dehumanizes not only the object of wrath, but the subject. In ire, we lose our reasoning either to rationalizing and equivocation about our impeccably justified anger or just to the overwhelming response of passion. As clear thinking becomes the puppet of wrath, we ourselves become the puppet of whatever is inflaming that wrath. I become the guy with the end table on his head. I become the doglike man stabbing himself. I can't forget the summation of wrath by Frederick Buechner, one of my favorite twentieth-century authors:

> Of the Seven Deadly Sins, anger is possibly the most fun. To lick your wounds, to smack your lips over grievances long past, to roll over your tongue the prospect of bitter confrontations still to come, to savor to the last toothsome morsel both the pain you are given and the pain you are giving back—in many ways, it is a feast fit for a king. The chief drawback is that what you are wolfing down is yourself. The skeleton at the feast is you.[24]

All wrath initially manifests as violence toward others. In the end, wrath is also violence toward the self. Wrath "wasteth and destroyeth the likeness of God."[25]

---

23. British Library Add. MS 18850, Bedford Hours 96r, accessed September 23, 2023, https://www.bl.uk/manuscripts/Viewer.aspx?ref=add_ms_18850_fs001ar.

24. Frederick Buechner, *Wishful Thinking: A Theological ABC* (San Francisco: Harper & Row, 1973), 2.

25. Chaucer, *Parson*, l. 543.

Hammered Gold, Harrowed Fields, Crushed Peppercorns

There is no one agreed-upon traditional "remedy" to wrath in medieval discussions of the seven capital vices. Instead, there are many: patience, meekness, knowledge (not a habit, so not a virtue, but a gift of the Spirit), and funny little medieval virtues like "evenhead" that did not make it into modern English. For the sake of space here, I will focus on meekness and patience. If wrath wastes and destroys the likeness of God through violence done to others and the self, its remedies—meekness and patience in particular—preserve and enhance humanity's likeness to God through the habitual rejection of violence. But meekness and patience remain tricky words. Let's think about patience first, for it is the mother of meekness.

In James 1:4 in the Middle English Bible, we learn that "soothly patience hath a perfect work, that ye be perfect and whole, in nothing failing."[26] Thomas Aquinas comments on this passage: "Patience is said to have a perfect work in bearing hardships: for these give rise first to sorrow, which is moderated by patience; second, to anger, which is moderated by meekness."[27] In patience, as we endure the suffering of some external event, we discern large evils from smaller ones and modulate our behavior accordingly. An angry reaction while stuck in traffic is different from an angry reaction while witnessing or experiencing discrimination. Yet even anger in a righteous cause needs patience by its side because it can still embitter a soul or be expressed through returning cruelty.

---

26. Middle English translation of the Vulgate, *Wycliffe's Bible*, ed. Josiah Forshall and Frederic Madden (Oxford, UK: Oxford University Press, 1850).

27. *ST* II-II.136.2.ad1.

There are two important things to know about patience. First, as with all virtues, one starts to acquire it through small things, like waiting in line at the grocery store without snapping at the checkout clerk who has badly bungled the situation, or kindly correcting your friend's idiocy rather than biting their head off. If someone has never been patient in little things, how can they become patient in big things, like marital conflict or parenting teenagers or bodily hardship?

The second thing is that we have been badly habituated into thinking of patience as passivity. Shut up and take it; become a statue in response to evil or misfortune. The white moderate pastors of the 1950s and '60s took Martin Luther King Jr. to task for his "impatience," arguing that the system would change naturally and all he needed to do was wait *patiently*.[28] We are told Job is both meek and patient. But he does not scruple to angrily or sorrowfully question the Lord or call out his friends for their stupid interpretations of the awful events that have befallen him (Job 21). In the long arc of history, we have witnessed that King's patience—action in nonviolence in the face of evil—was true patience, unlike the passivity counseled to him. In a little fifteenth-century treatise with the evocative name of *The Tree and the Twelve Fruits of the Holy Ghost*, the author writes that "patience ordains us to the fruition and use of endless peace."[29] Dr. King's patience was nothing like the fake patience of passivity, but instead showed the fruits of a heart ordained to the fruition

28. Martin Luther King, Jr., "Letter from Birmingham Jail," accessed September 20, 2023, https://www.csuchico.edu/iege/_assets/documents/susi-letter-from-birmingham-jail.pdf.

29. *A deuout treatyse called the tree & xii. frutes of the holy goost: Edited from MS McClean 132*, ed. J. J. Vaissier (Groningen: J.B. Wolters, 1960), 73.

and use of peace in patient working toward a world more peaceful because it is more just. Sometimes patience does look similar to stillness and waiting, and sometimes it does not.

Our old friend Bishop William writes of a Patience who rhapsodizes about her role in the life of goodness. Patience tells her readers she is like a hammered gold vessel: If the misshapen gold knew its maker, knew what it was about to become, it would welcome the contortion and flames and hammering it takes in the service of beauty. Patience is like rare and expensive peppercorns that have traveled all the way from the Far East only to be crushed—which increases their power to flavor dish after dish. Patience is like wheat being ground into wholesome bread. Patience is like the tilled ground, harrowed and open, where tender shoots will sprout without the barrier of hardened soil. I can continue this list without the help of William: Patience is the new life that comes from bodies, where organs have been squished into weird corners, joints have come loose, blood has been lost; patience is the wine that comes forth from the grapes flattened in the winepress and compressed into barrels for years; patience is the caterpillar weaving what seems like its own tomb, only to emerge as something that can fly. In patience, something feels unbearably hard, and nothing will be the same again—not your body, not the lump of gold, not the grapes, not even the peppercorn. But then something else happens that you could not have foreseen if you had never seen it before, and a new taste, a new shape, a new person is born. This collection of images holds in uncomfortable tension the beauty that can emerge only from forms of broken life. In patience, we bear the broken and jagged pieces of the hard parts of our lives, in big and little things, in trust that Christ is working our redemption. Patience, as a response to difficulty and suffering, is one of those virtues that will not exist in the kingdom of heaven. But here and now it is a necessity for humans, who will inevitably face the trials of hardship and death.

A Pillow for the Soul

As a particular kind of patience in times of anger, meekness is the remedy that especially ministers against the poison of wrath. But as my examples earlier showed, this is a virtue that in modernity we are more likely to think of as a vice. Why does Christ exhort and model meekness? What *is* meekness? Here's one strange medieval answer: a pillow. One medieval manual for priests on the vices and virtues, the *Summa virtutum de remediis anime*, says, "Meekness is the soft pillow on the bed of conscience, on which our soul rests in safety."[30] Unlike wrath, causing one to toss and turn, unable to rest, meekness offers space for rest even in conflict. Meekness entails a disposition for peace, an inherent turning to peace in the face of anger, as wrath is an ingrained habit of turning toward force. In Thomas Aquinas's words, "Meekness moderates anger according to right reason," regulating the desire for vengeance, destroying hatred itself.[31] In Psalm 37:11, the psalm Jesus alludes to in his Beatitudes, the psalmist writes, "The meek shall inherit the land and delight themselves in abundant prosperity," for which older translations use "the abundance of peace" (KJV).

30. *Summa virtutum de remediis anime*, ed. and trans. by Siegfried Wenzel (Athens, GA: University of Georgia Press, 1984), 154.

31. *ST* II-II.157.2.r.

Meekness is confusing because we English-speakers have occasionally used it as a synonym for humility.[32] Humility is at the root of meekness, just as it is at the root of the other true virtues. But meekness is not the virtue of self-knowledge, it is the virtue of gentleness and mildness, the habitual resistance to provocation and egoism. The *Summa virtutum* quotes the Greek father Saint John Chrysostom: "Meekness is the calmness of a mind which cannot be easily vexed by the evils it suffers nor be provoked to inflict evils."[33] Note, according to Chrysostom, how meekness is not a wholesale rejection of anger, but its practice means one cannot be "easily vexed." In fact, one begins to see the relationship between meekness and anger: Meekness, too, is a form of resistance in the soul, a power, a presence, an agency.

And what does this presence, this inclination for a gentle response do? "Meekness disposes man to the knowledge of God, by removing an obstacle; and this in two ways. First, because it makes man self-possessed by mitigating his anger . . . second, because it pertains to meekness that a man does not contradict the words of truth, which many do through being disturbed by anger."[34] Meekness makes room for truth to work in the soul. Humility's knowledge turns inward; meekness's knowledge turns outward. For nothing stymies false anger and nothing feeds virtuous anger more than knowledge.[35] *The Book of Vices and Virtues* notes that the gift of knowledge often casts out wrath. Knowledge has the

---

32. Meekness is often used by Middle English speakers instead of humility for the concept of humility. But it is not the Latin *humilitas*; it is closer to the Latin *mitis* or *mansuetus*, the words that older translations, like the KJV and the Douay-Rheims, select "meekness" to translate.

33. *Summa virtutum*, 152.

34. Thomas Aquinas, *ST* II-II.157.4.ad1.

35. Knowledge is often listed as a medieval remedy for anger, but it is a gift of the Holy Spirit rather than a habit.

potential to make men and women wiser and more measured in all things. Again, the psalms remind us, "The meek will he guide in judgment: and the meek will he teach his way" (Ps. 25:9 KJV). *The Book of Vices and Virtues* describes this gift of knowledge in architectural imagery: One becomes like the master builder of cathedrals, who knows the measures, who doesn't miss a line or a levelling. *The Book* also announces that with this gift one becomes more like the angels of the Lord, who are "all full of eyes to-fore and behind."[36] Sign me up! I could read two books at once. But in seriousness, who hasn't prematurely flared up in wrath to discover mitigating circumstances—what *really* happened. A friend is late to lunch, you're ticked off because your time is limited, then you discover that the friend was in a car accident or had an awful morning. With increased knowledge, wrath dissipates.

Hatred too—"Old wrath"—can be shattered by the revelations of measured knowledge. A recent book by Eli Saslow, *Rising Out of Hatred,* depicts the transformation of the white supremacist wunderkind Derek Black. Black attended college, and some brave Jewish students befriended him. The power of their friendship and the newfound knowledge about Jewish people that Black was confronted with firsthand challenged his hatred to its core and led him to publicly renounce white supremacy and caused his family and community to reject him. Black's hatred could not bear the light of truth.

Additionally, knowledge can fruitfully increase anger when necessary. When the anger of the meek is aroused, it is all the more powerful in its foundation of peace and eschewing of violence. Yet knowledge on its own is not enough to challenge wrath.

---

36. *Book,* 149.

And often we learn too late—after the storm of wrath has already destroyed something valuable. Knowledge is only given the power of transformation in the space in our souls and bodies kept by meekness and patience.

A Virtue for the Powerful

Why the repeated scriptural insistence that the meek inherit the earth? Is this a reference to the coming kingdom of heaven, which we anticipate? Yes and no. Meekness, wrote medieval thinkers, should be especially *a virtue for the powerful.*

That took a surprising turn—completely counter to the examples of so-called meekness with which I began this chapter! It turns out that our modern "meekness" bears as much relation to Christlike meekness as mud to expensive chocolate. They occasionally look similar outwardly, but their taste and purpose are nothing alike. Meekness is for *all* who follow the path of Christ, who in that path are relearning how to wield power. But it is particularly recommended not to those we have historically and badly recommended it to—enslaved people, women, the oppressed, children—but especially to those who find themselves born to power, in historical positions of power, or increasing their influence through their work. Wrath and power, as we are reminded, are extremely dangerous bedfellows. Violence is the condition of humankind, as Simone Weil reminds us in her exquisite reading of *The Iliad.*[37] The more power you have, the greater your capacity for force.

37. Please read Simone Weil, "*The Iliad*, or the Poem of Force," translated by Mary McCarthy, *Politics* (1945), accessed January 15, 2025, https://archive.org/details/iliador-poemoffor00simo. .

The *Summa virtutum* states, "Meekness *deserves to be a leader.*"[38] Only the meek are not purely reactive in their contexts; they alone can reject an eye for an eye and a tooth for a tooth and break the perpetual cycle of violence. A meek person is a free person, the only truly free person. The meek inherit the earth because they are the only ones who can be trusted with that kingly inheritance. Only meek Mary is mother of Jesus. Only the meek Jesus can judge hearts; only the mild Savior can rule the world. But neither practiced the kind of watery meekness we have come to expect and dread.

Oh, the meek turn the other cheek and reject wrath, all right, and the world roundly punishes them for it. The ironic epigram attributed to J. Paul Getty, midcentury oil baron and billionaire, is true: The meek won't be getting mineral rights; they won't become billionaires. Their inheritance does look different. Christ the King is the meek lamb who did not open his mouth before the slaughter. We witness his crucifixion as the great final rejection of humanity's wasting wrath. But we also see Jesus flip tables, we see him call out religious leadership, we see him heal the ill and speak to the outcast and violate social taboos.

We adore mild Mary, meek mother who weeps with those who weep. But meek Mary is also *Theotokos*, God-bearer, singer of the Magnificat:

> My soul magnifies the Lord,
> and my spirit rejoices in God my Savior,
> for he has looked with favor on the lowly state of
> his servant.

38. *Summa virtutum*, 156. Italics mine.

> Surely from now on all generations will call
> me blessed,
> for the Mighty One has done great things for me,
> and holy is his name;
> indeed, his mercy is for those who fear him
> from generation to generation.
> He has shown strength with his arm;
> he has scattered the proud in the imagination
> of their hearts.
> He has brought down the powerful from their thrones
> and lifted up the lowly;
> he has filled the hungry with good things
> and sent the rich away empty.
> He has come to the aid of his child Israel,
> in remembrance of his mercy,
> according to the promise he made to our ancestors,
> to Abraham and to his descendants forever.
> (Luke 1:46–55)

That doesn't sound very milky mild. Or we read James 5, where the rich are lambasted and excoriated—and then in the very next paragraph, we are exhorted to be patient and mild in our sufferings and anger.

The truly meek person chooses to suffer rather than inflict violence—perhaps to his death. The meek person is diametrically opposed to hatred in that she truly possesses the vision of Christ: She sees the *imago Dei* even at her angriest, even in the faces of the worst foes. The meek do not wilt under pressure, submitting to oppression because they are too weak to fight back. Only the meek are courageous and loving and powerful enough to refuse to return violence in the face of the sword that pierces the soul and the nails that perforate the hands and feet. No wonder we rarely witness meekness. No wonder we are so collectively terrified of and disturbed by it that we have reduced it semantically to timidity or cowardice.

This all sounds impossible, and maybe even naive. I realize I have come full circle, back to throwing roses at Wrath, who is not armed with flowers but with a sword already stained with blood. I am not meek. I seethe at minor slights and cherish a good deal of bitterness. But I—and you, too—have witnessed real meekness, and it is undeniably beautiful and laden with a power I don't fully understand.

In Christ, in Mary, in the great servants of God like Stephen, or Perpetua and Felicity, or Saint Óscar Romero, or Martin Luther King Jr. and his fellow participants in radical nonviolence and civil disobedience, or the monks of Tibhirine, we meet the utter and total refusal of force, patience and meekness, the orientation of the heart for peace. These aren't just any roses that drive away Wrath; they are blossoms *of the cross*. In fact, meekness and patience are perhaps *the* distinctive Christian virtues, the Christlike virtues that truly set Christians apart from the cultures they inhabit. The truly meek are fearfully farseeing and otherworldly. They are the crushed peppercorns in the dish, the vessels of thin-hammered gold, the harrowed ground where new green comes.

Practices and Prayer

> Be still before the Lord, and wait patiently for him;
> do not fret over those who prosper in their way,
> over those who carry out evil devices.

Refrain from anger and forsake wrath.
Do not fret—it leads only to evil.
For the wicked shall be cut off,
but those who wait for the LORD shall inherit the land.

Yet a little while, and the wicked will be no more;
though you look diligently for their place, they will not be there.
But the meek shall inherit the land
and delight themselves in abundant prosperity. (Ps. 37:7–11)

Practices

- Pick a small way to resist wrath through patience and meekness. A few options: Take a deep breath before responding in conversation. Stop immediately posting on social media when you're angry—wait a day. Even silly things, like choosing the longest line at the checkout or refusing to cuss when someone cuts you off can be welcome baby steps into an orientation toward peace.
- Reflect on these questions with a trusted friend, family member, or spouse:
  - *What typically makes me angry?*
  - *Where have I seen the difference between patience and passivity in my own life or the lives around me?*
- Read further on patience and meekness: "Letter from Birmingham Jail" by Martin Luther King, Jr., *The Hiding Place* by Corrie ten Boom, *Godric* by Frederick Buechner.

Prayer

Lord Jesus, make me meek, with the meekness of the roses of the cross. I know this is a costly thing to ask and that it will come only with the trials that lead to patience. As I face these difficult situations, help me to reject anger that morphs into wrath and welcome the anger that rectifies injustice. Give me discernment that I may not confuse the two. Thank you for the space given by meekness and patience that allows new knowledge to guide my anger, and aid me to cultivate that space in my responses. Reorient my heart toward the peace that passes human understanding. Amen.

CHAPTER FIVE

SLOTH AND FORTITUDE: SNAIL AND SANDALS

"I will go at once, Father. But you should not be discouraged; one does not die of a cold." The old man smiled. "I shall not die of a cold, my son. I shall die of having lived."

—Willa Cather, *Death Comes for the Archbishop*

Let us not grow weary in doing what is right, for we will reap at harvest time, if we do not give up.

—Galatians 6:9

In a crumbling manuscript within the ancient archives of Oxford, one encounters a curious set of fourteenth-century poems facing each other. One long-dead Middle English word links them together. One poem is a plea from Christ on the cross to the onlookers below the cross, at the moment of his death, or more pertinently, to those looking upon his suffering in art or imagination. Christ says:

> Man and woman, look to me,
> How much pain I suffered [*tholed*] for thee;
> Look upon my back, how sore I was beaten;
> Look to my side, what blood have I shed;
> My feet and my hands are nailed to the rood
> [cross];
> From the thorns pricking my head runs the
> blood;
> From side to side, from head to the foot,
> Turn my body about, overall thou findest blood.
> Man, thine heart, thine heart, turn it to me,
> For the Five Wounds I suffered [*tholed*] for thee.[1]

These addresses from the suffering Christ were a frequent theme in Middle English poetry.

---

1. My translation of New College, Oxford MS. 88, f. 179. Punctuation and text in *Religious Lyrics of the XIVth Century*, ed. Carleton Brown (Oxford: Oxford University Press, 1924), 3.

On the facing page dwells a short, haunting poem from the same time. Rather than God speaking to humanity, now we eavesdrop on a person speaking to God:

> Lord, you called me
> And I did not answer you
> Except in words slow and sleepy:
> "Wait [*thole*] yet! Wait [*thole*] a little!"
> But "yet" and "yet" was endless,
> And "*thole* a little" a long way is.[2]

This poem translates part of Saint Augustine's *Confessions*. In Book VIII, on the cusp of conversion, Augustine is "weighed down by the pleasant burden of the world in the way one commonly is by sleep," and even as he hears in different ways, *Arise, sleeper, rise from the dead,* he has no answer but the drowsy "just a minute."[3] Yet a minute can stretch to endlessness. Such sluggishness has long been associated with the spiritual vice of sloth.[4]

Today sloth is sometimes associated with simple laziness. It is treated as the joke-worthy Homer Simpson of the seven capital vices. In what world is slumping on the couch, taking long naps,

---

2. My translation of New College, Oxford MS. 88, f. 179. Punctuation and text in *Religious Lyrics of the XIVth Century*, 3.

3. Augustine, *Confessions*, trans. Maria Boulding, O.S.B. (New York: New City Press, 1997), VIII.5.

4. Sloth is associated with the ancient vice of *acedia*, but there are some differences. For more on early conceptions of *acedia*, see Rebecca Konyndyk DeYoung's *Glittering Vices: A New Look at the Seven Deadly Sins and Their Remedies*, 2nd ed. (Grand Rapids: Brazos, 2020), ch. 5. Occasionally, critics and writers have paired acedia with clinical depression. But this unhelpfully conflates vice—a habitual albeit ingrained choice—with illness. People with clinical depression are no saintlier than anyone else, so I'm sure many of them struggle with sloth. But it is confusing and damaging to conflate illness and vice, though they often work together in oppression of our minds and bodies.

and watching bad television a deadly serious sin? It's really only a sin against the grinding gears of capitalism, the half-charming habit of a sitcom dad! Such behavior presents a problem for cleaning the kitchen or reading medieval philosophy, but a vicious root of moral disorder? Come on.

Yet in the pairing of these lyrics, we discover elements to sloth deeper than silly puritanical resistance to relaxing. The Middle English word *thole* appears repeatedly in both pieces, making the poems two voices in a conversation. The *thole* of the first means "to suffer, to endure."[5] For you I *thole,* Christ says directly to the reader. He pleads, *turn to me, turn to me.* Christ bears the suffering of the cross in obedience to his great love for humanity. As Saint Augustine so beautifully wrote, "Fortitude is love bearing all things readily for the sake of the beloved."[6] Jesus acts in fortitude, sloth's remedy.[7]

The *thole* of the second poem shifts a little. It means "to wait." The slothful heart answers "thole a litel," *wait just a moment more.* Sloth habitually dodges our true vocation of love, with God or with our neighbor or even ourselves, because this call challenges our hearts and habits. We respond, like the speaker of the poem, *I am not ready to change my ways. I want to do what I want to do.* Contrasted with the first *thole,* this second *thole* becomes

---

5. *Middle English Dictionary,* "tholen" (n.), accessed January 17, 2024, https://quod.lib.umich.edu/m/middle-english-dictionary/dictionary/MED45378/track?counter=12&search_id=74839374.

6. Saint Augustine, *On the Morals of the Catholic Church,* trans. Richard Stothert, from *Nicene and Post-Nicene Fathers, First Series,* vol. 4, ed. Philip Schaff (Buffalo, NY: Christian Literature, 1887). Revised and edited for New Advent by Kevin Knight, accessed January 28, 2024, http://www.newadvent.org/fathers/1401.htm.

7. The Middle English word often used to name sloth's remedy virtue is *strength,* a synonym for fortitude. I use fortitude instead to avoid our modern exclusive connotations with physical strength.

an unfeeling and even ironic dismissal of suffering. In the contrast between the two uses, readers' eyes are suddenly opened to the centuries of tension between the suffering and the sleepily comfortable—the impassioned "tholing" of one and callous "thole a little longer" of the other. Rather than laziness, sloth closely resembles spiritual apathy or even cowardice.

Things Left Undone

Escaping the specter of sitcom-dad sloth is difficult and not only confined to modernity. The penitential work *Jacob's Well,* always to be counted on for colorful and sometimes questionable examples of the vice or virtue at hand, tells the story of a hermit living a long walk from his water source. He moved his shelter closer to a brook so he would not have to walk as far. But as it turned out, angels were counting his footsteps to calculate the merit of his hermithood. Alas! He then moved back to the farther spot, which nicely solved both his sloth and merit problems (a lot more steps for the angels to count). Is this really sloth? Could the answer really just be to work more and harder?[8]

Part of the conceptual difficulty of sloth is that sloth is often a vice of spiritual omission. Making a task more laborious for labor's sake or more painful for pain's sake does not usually solve a problem of the spirit. In the Book of Common Prayer, the prayer

---

8. *Jacob's Well* is a fifteenth-century text. Scholars like Morton Bloomfield see this example in *Jacob's Well* as evidence that sloth was losing its status as a serious vice by then and moving toward our modern understanding of it as laziness; *The Seven Deadly Sins: An Introduction to the History of a Religious Concept, with Special Reference to Medieval English Literature* (Michigan State University Press, 1952, reprint 1967), 223.

of confession famously acknowledges, "We have left undone those things which we ought to have done, and we have done those things which we ought not to have done, and there is no health in us."[9] Coldness, slackness, neglect, avoidance, or even outright refusal all characterize the life of sloth. The Israelites refuse to enter the promised land because they are afraid of how hard the conquering of the land will be. Peter denies Christ. People leave their children or spouse. But it can be smaller actions too: I do not bother to text or call a friend back; I stop praying regularly because it feels dull. Sometimes my family's needs are so demanding that I hide myself, figuratively, in books and thoughts and distance, like Mr. Bennet in *Pride and Prejudice*.

The Book of Vices and Virtues calls sloth "weariness of good deeds."[10] A slothful person dares not go down a path, says the *Book*, for "fear of a snail that showeth his horns." He is like a child who runs away "from a goose that hisseth." In other words, sloth occurs when we are so daunted by an obstacle, big or small, that we simply choose to avoid an action or purpose or person altogether, even though we know that by doing so we err in love. This sleepwalking through life won't usually be solved by moving one's shelter farther away from a water source.

If you're like me, burned out by the pandemic and parenting small children and terrifying foreign wars and disastrous cultural discourse and fear about the environment (and so on), you might be dazedly thinking, "What's wrong with the easy way? Lord, give me easiness, I beg." I would like a cozy hobbit-hole life. There is

9. "An ordre for Morning prayer dayly throughout the yere," the Book of Common Prayer (1559), ed. Brian Cummings (Oxford, 2011), 103.

10. *The Book of Vices and Virtues: A Fourteenth Century English Translation of the Somme Le Roi of Lorens d'Orleans*, ed. W. Nelson Francis (Oxford: Oxford University Press, 1998), 26.

nothing wrong with this desire, with ease itself or relaxing. Rest is a gift of God *necessary* to a whole human. The spiritual practice of sabbath-keeping teaches humans the lovely necessity of rest. In margins, space, and quiet we learn to reject the thin worldly wail for productivity and distraction. So sloth is not about too much rest. Instead, sloth concerns a person learning to value ease over everything else in their actions. The Carmelite friar Richard Lavynham defined sloth as "a vice which is rooted in the person uneager [or *unlusty,* as he more vividly puts it] to serve God or the world, desiring no other bliss but ease alone."[11]

Prizing ease over all other goods exacts a shockingly high cost in relationships, whether those are with God, with other humans, even with the land.[12] And relationships are what we are called to as the children of God and the body of Christ. We are born into relationships that preexist us and baptized into a body of tissues and veins that transcends time and place. Philosopher Rebecca Konyndyk DeYoung describes the costs of choosing ease within Saint Thomas Aquinas's understanding of sloth: "Slothful people want all the comforts of being in a relationship—with the identity, security, love, and happiness it brings—while ultimately resisting or refusing to let love change them or make disciples of them. They are like a married couple who long for a relationship of unconditional love, but who chafe at the thought of disciplining their own desires or sacrificing themselves in order to maintain that relationship and allow it to flourish."[13]

---

11. Richard Lavynham, *A Litil Tretys,* ed. J. P. W. M. van Zutphen (Rome: Institutum Carmelitanum, 1956), 15.

12. I think we are only beginning to see the horrors of the West's slothful attitude toward the earth, in eagerness to wreck whatever we please in pursuit of pleasure and ease.

13. DeYoung, *Glittering Vices,* 192.

This resistance to the demands of life together varies according to individual temperaments. For some, this avoidance or distraction looks like passivity or indolence. For others, it looks like overbusyness and "too great a zeal," in the words of the medieval writers, for fasting, cluttered schedules, and spiritual practices that end up being just another attempt to claw our way out of what we are actually asked to do in love.[14]

Yet these digressions end similarly. Sloth in all its shapes leads to self-contempt and restless, bone-deep unhappiness. The slothful one becomes increasingly callous to beauty, to ugliness, to need, to love itself—in service to her own desire for ease. A devastating account of sloth from the pen of William of Saint-Thierry, monk and friend of Saint Bernard of Clairvaux, clarifies the vice's stakes. He describes his own deadness to beauty, dullness to love, despair itself: "Long persistence in bad ways, along with very great insensibility of mind, has hardened me. I have learned to sleep with the sunshine full on my face, and have grown used to it; I have become accustomed to not seeing what takes place before my eyes and, dead at heart as I am, though I am set in the midst of the sea, I have ceased to hear the roaring of its waves and the thunder of the sky."[15]

His insensibility was not the result of disability or weariness or bad fortune. Instead, William's voice echoing from a thousand years back tells of how he learned to ignore the love notes of God, whether they arrived in quiet beauty or resplendent fearful glory. "But as for me, I have rotted on earth,"[16] agonized William. We avoid the garden snail in the path, only to discover that it

14. *Book*, 27.

15. William of Saint-Thierry, *Meditations*, trans. A Religious of C.S.M.V. (New York: Harper & Brothers, 1954), 20.

16. William of St-Thierry, *Meditations*, 19.

has grown monstrous in size the longer we avoid it. A habit of spiritual avoidance can easily become despair.

Despair's essence is revealed in its Middle English name: *wanhope,* or lack-hope, un-hope. Sloth can't bring itself to believe that love is real and worth its challenge. A heart accustomed to ignoring even one's own challenging desires in favor of easier things ceases hoping in love's final victory.

But fortitude, the cousin to hope, a virtue born in human vulnerability and need, stands against those final fruits of sloth.

Sandals and Roads

The most common Middle English word for sloth's remedy virtue is *strength.* Yet this word creates too much confusion for us today. We think of strength as the antithesis to weakness. In moments of defeat, crisis, and pain, I think, "I wish I were braver; I wish I were stronger." But the ancient virtue of *strength* is possible only in vulnerability. The Latin word for this remedy virtue is *fortitudo,* the root of our modern fortitude, which is the word I use in this chapter instead. It is a word long allied with courage and endurance. Thomas Aquinas writes of fortitude as the virtue that removes obstacles, specifically bodily obstacles, to doing the right thing.[17] This is rather abstract. He means we will face frightening, daunting, tiring, or even tedious challenges in this life. And fortitude moderates our fear and exhaustion around these difficulties, the greatest of which is death.[18] We fear death in all its

17. *ST* II-II.123.1.r.
18. *ST* II-II.123.4.r.

forms. We fear the death of our bodies or the death of loved ones or the death of a dream or home or friendship or success. We fear what Stanley Hauerwas calls the "little death" of every unknown: those little deaths we face all the time, every day in dying to ego, facing mystery or lack of control.[19] Fortitude enables us to face these little deaths with courage and constancy as we pursue the life of love together in Jesus.

It does not dispel our fears entirely. Total fearlessness is not a virtue, but rather a vice named recklessness. However, fortitude helps us learn when to listen to fear, when to preserve our bodies or ourselves, and when to move forward anyway in the threat or presence of loss. Fortitude occurs only in our vulnerability.

Fortitude can show up as specific actions of courage. The soldier or knight in battle has represented courage all the way back to Aristotle.[20] But it is more likely, writes Aquinas, to show up as endurance. In a beautiful phrase, Aquinas writes that endurance is "an action of the soul cleaving resolutely to good."[21] Less glamorous than knights in shining armor, fortitude resembles a pair of sandals, tells one medieval sermon collection.[22] We are pilgrims on the road to the kingdom of heaven. Fortitude keeps us trudging along, taking some of the ache away from weary feet.

In classic medieval fashion (how they loved lists of all kinds!), some commentators listed types of fortitude progressively, like

---

19. Stanley Hauerwas, *The Character of Virtue: Letters to a Godson* (Eerdmans, 2018), 113.

20. Knighthood is by far the dominant metaphor in medieval writings on spiritual strength or fortitude. But I have written at length about this before and did not want to cover the same ground—see *Jesus through Medieval Eyes*, ch. 4.

21. *ST* II-II.123.7.ad2.

22. *Fasciculus Morum: A Fourteenth-Century Preacher's Handbook*, ed. and trans. Siegfried Wenzel (University Park, PA: The Pennsylvania State University Press, 1989), 263.

steps on a journey. When we first step out on a journey, we do so in vision and hope, the first category of fortitude called greatheartedness. This is the voluntary and reasonable undertaking of difficult things. This willingness to dream, plan, and act where others see only certain failure constitutes those first steps of fortitude.

To continue along the way, we practice confidence, which may surprise those who only associate medieval writers with groveling and self-flagellating. It may take greatheartedness to begin something, but it takes confidence to keep going. Confidence's companion on the middle way is composure, "not to be afraid of the inconveniences that lie before us and accompany the task we have begun."[23] In confidence and composure, one trusts that the road may be long but that the call of love is real.

Finally, there are the kinds of courage required for the end of the road. We practice the part of fortitude called high-mindedness, "carrying difficult and noble things to the end."[24] This virtue takes pride in a job well done, in welcoming and attending to the bits and pieces that one could ignore in the end. But the last road virtue of all is particularly meaningful to me: constancy, "the mind's stability that is firm and persevering in its resolve."[25] I named my third child Constance. She was born in the very beginning of the COVID-19 pandemic. I was afflicted by pre- and postpartum anxiety exacerbated by the deep and crippling fear we all lived in. For me, her name, chosen long before we were in quarantine, became a hope for myself. Constancy

23. *Summa virtutum*, 238.

24. *Summa virtutum*, 238.

25. *Summa virtutum*, 240.

"makes the heart as steadfast and trusty to God as the tower that is founded upon the hard rock."[26] It cannot be taken in battle.

The Anvil

An illuminated manuscript at Oxford wonderfully and weirdly brings this enduring fortitude to life.[27] Fortitude, in a common trope of the day, is drawn as a young woman. She stands amid a group of other women. Upon her head rests something surreal and strange: an anvil. Yes, the heavy object that blacksmiths hammer on as they make horseshoes and door hinges, or the hunk of metal that flattens Wile E. Coyote in his fruitless attempts to catch the Road Runner. Lady Fortitude bears the anvil carefully atop her braided blonde tresses.

This anvil represents the weight of external circumstances that each person faces in her unique context as she learns to cleave to good, to love Jesus, herself, and her neighbor. Sometimes this anvil is specific, very heavy, even horrible: battling illness or facing past trauma or loss. Fortitude resists despair in the face of these anvil-like outward circumstances. This resistance does not necessarily make the anvil less heavy. At times each of us will feel utterly crushed, destroyed by the hardships of life. Sometimes bearing the anvil in fortitude is as simple and difficult as getting out of bed in the morning (or staying in bed to heal).

Though we often associate fortitude with the prolonged battles of loss or illness or war, sometimes just living is exhausting. Working, parenting, moving, loving a particular family member, or finishing

26. *Book*, 168.

27. Bodley MS. Laud misc. 570, fol. 21v.

The Master of Sir John Falstof, "Lady Fortitude," manuscript illumination, ca. 1450, Bodley MS. Laud misc. 570, fol. 21v., Bodleian Libraries, Oxford. © Bodleian Libraries, University of Oxford

a project can be really hard. Again, Augustine writes, "Fortitude is love bearing all things readily for the sake of the beloved."[28] *For the sake of the beloved.* We should not labor under anvils that are not ours—not out of guilt or to be more impressive or because we are afraid of disappointing someone. Each person bears only the anvils

28. Saint Augustine, *On the Morals of the Catholic Church,* trans. Richard Stothert, from *Nicene and Post-Nicene Fathers, First Series,* vol. 4, ed. Philip Schaff (Buffalo, NY: Christian Literature, 1887). Revised and edited for New Advent by Kevin Knight, accessed January 28, 2024, http://www.newadvent.org/fathers/1401.htm.

into which he is called as he follows Christ deeper into relationships, those with God, with himself, with neighbors and enemies.

None of us are called into a life of being a doormat, but all relationships require specific moments when one must submit one's own comfort and desires to what the circumstances ask, for the sake of love. Waking up in the middle of the night, night after night, is not easy, but it is necessary when I have an infant. I do not love exercising. But it is part of loving my body well and recognizing it as a gift from God. Taking responsibility for a mistake I made at work is humiliating but part of learning. Showing up for a friend who needs me when I am tired is an act of faithful love. We learn and practice fortitude daily in a hallowed tenacity, sanctified stubbornness, faithful presence, when it would be far easier to hide, run, or grow embittered.

The Dragon in the Castle

Besides bearing the anvil on her head, Lady Fortitude holds another odd object in her arms: a diminutive castle. Face intent, she pulls *a dragon* out from the archway door of this tiny keep. The castle or fortress has long been a symbol for the soul, and fortitude is a virtuous practice not only in the outward circumstances of our lives. One of the most important parts of fortitude is the capacity it gives us to face the dragons inside ourselves, in our own hearts.

Sloth can take the form of a deep dread that one's sins are too foul, too big, too powerful. One avoids, at all costs, looking within to discover that serpentine self. This dread takes place individually *and* corporately. Such avoidance both in Christ's body and in our own self-examinations allows you and me to excuse ourselves from accountability. Yet that hunger and thirst for righteousness must extend within. It requires great courage and painful endurance to confront those dragons. And so, though at first it struck me as wildly strange, it makes sense that in the middle of many medieval discussions of fortitude one finds lengthy digressions on the sacrament of penance.[29]

Lest, at the mention of medieval penance, your mind immediately goes to *Monty Python* monks thumping themselves in the face with Bibles, this sacrament was historically rooted in reconciliation and community, not plain self-punishment. Traditionally, there were three steps in this sacrament: repentance in heart, confession of mouth, and satisfaction in deeds. Self-examination, repentance, and reconciliation are some of the hardest, scariest vocations Christians face in life together. They necessitate the same holy resolve that outward challenges require. All dragons must be evicted. And it's not enough simply to recognize that you have sinned, argued medieval theologians and penitential manuals. For healing to occur, both within and without, action must be taken in these three steps.

First, repentance in heart, also called contrition, is heartfelt, true sorrow over what one has done or failed to do. The preacher's handbook *Fasciculus morum* notes that God is close to the humble and contrite heart (Ps. 51:17). Then the compiler uses two rather jarring examples in tandem: Christ is like a falcon who has caught a little bird in hunting, like "mankind as his prey from the field of hell."[30] In falconry, the ancient practice of hunting with birds of prey, the falcon is then given the bird's heart as a reward, cut into

29. Check out the *Fasciculus morum*, where the section on *accidia* suddenly becomes a lecture on penance, or *The Book of Vices and Virtues*, where fourteen pages on repentance sit smack dab in the middle of fortitude!

30. *Fasciculus morum*, 439.

pieces and cleansed, as in contrition and confession. "Rend your hearts," commands the prophet Joel in repentance, and then these hearts are gifts to God himself.

This bloody example is paired with another. God is like a mother or a nurse running to her crying child. While the child sleeps in the crib, the mother goes about her tasks, but when the child cries out, she immediately leaves her task to embrace the baby.[31] In learning how to regret and lament over individual and corporate sins, we are both the lovingly cradled, crying child and the bleeding heart. Real pain over what we have done *and* the full knowledge of secure love coexist in real repentance, for "his tender mercies are over all his works" (Ps. 145:9 KJV).

However, contrition should not be confused with self-hatred. Self-hatred in sin's aftermath is futile. Self-hatred never heals—not me, not the person I hurt. It offers nothing to God, who eternally loves what he has created. Though *I* feel contrition over a way I have sinned against God or humankind, my contrition is not circular and self-referential, like self-loathing. Repentance is generative. In my regret over how I have hurt myself and others, I trust the love of God as I confess what I have done or left undone.

The second step of this process of penance is confession of sin. For medieval Christians, confession was valid if it was full (no omitting parts of sins), completed in a timely fashion (don't wait your whole life), and made to a priest (say it out loud). Confession is necessary because in the great task of spiritual dragon-slaying, it is not enough to inwardly regret what I have done or failed to do. The marriage destroyed, the theft accomplished, the cruel words still echoing, the violence perpetuated—all remain unacknowledged

31. *Fasciculus morum*, 441.

without confession. Most of us do not want to confess, whether in its sacramental, priestly context or more generally in its form of a wholehearted and sorrowful acknowledgment and apology. But confession itself is an act of hopeful fortitude.

At last, the third step of penance is satisfaction in deeds. In the work of lasting repentance, contrition and confession lead to reparative action. Sometimes this is logical: If I steal something from you, I should not just apologize while quietly pocketing the profits. I ought to replace or pay for what I took to truly make amends. Other forms of satisfaction may be less obvious, like reshaping how you see God through prayer, relearning how to do hard things rather than take advantage of others, or publicly announcing your regret and sin. In the Middle Ages, satisfaction in deeds was set by one's priest and often took the form of prayers, pilgrimages, public penances like the stocks or whipping, or financial restitution, depending on the sin committed and the abilities of the sinner.[32] Some of these strike us as outlandish or harsh, at times damaging rather than healing. (Let's not return to public whippings.) However, at their best, these restitutions were meant to be part of a process of communal healing, of not merely papering over the wrongs we wreak upon one another. Satisfaction or restitution is the eager, humbling work of Zacchaeus in Luke 19:8: "Look, half of my possessions, Lord, I will give to the poor, and if I have defrauded anyone of anything, I will pay back four times as much." Jesus delights in this work of reunification of communities.

---

32. For more on medieval penance and the materials instructing it, see Thomas Tentler, *Sin and Confession on the Eve of the Reformation* (Princeton University Press, 1977); Eamon Duffy, *The Stripping of the Altars: Traditional Religion in England 1400–1580*, 2nd ed. (Yale University Press, 2005).

These processes of reconciliation are invitations into individual and communal transformation, by the grace of God. They are also costly and take a lot of courage. The heart of Christian fortitude beats not in combat nor defensiveness, not in medieval crusades nor in our modern silly imitation, the culture wars. It beats in dying to one's ego through the painful and continued journey of facing sins and weaknesses in love and honesty and learning how to reconcile and make amends. Fortitude, in its form of love bearing all for the beloved, will always lead us back to this holy labor of dragon-slaying.

Comfort in Fear: The Friends and the Winepress

Unsurprisingly, since fortitude always happens in vulnerability in regard to our fears, I too am afraid when I think of the tasks into which I am called. When I think of bearing anvils of love, of confession and reconciliation, something small and panicked in me cowers. Often we believe we're not being brave if we don't feel brave, or that we are not strong if we don't feel strong. But fortitude is not really about feelings; it is about presence. Many times I have heard friends say they need courage in the midst of hard things. But by choosing to just show up—in parenting, in reconstructing their life, in weathering the burdens of illness—they already begin the habit of fortitude.

It is important that I witness this in my friends, and they in me. For Lady Fortitude is not alone. Her companions, sister virtues like Perseverance, Constancy, and Patience, surround her. Fortitude is not solitary, shrouded in glorious individualism, lonely in its burdens, despite what many of us have culturally believed. "I must face this alone," we have heard countless heroes mutter in movies. Our burdens and tasks are of course *uniquely* our own, like Frodo's task as the Ring-bearer in *The Lord of the Rings*. But Frodo could not have cast the ring into the fires of Mount Doom without loyal Samwise Gamgee. From repentance to marriage, from self-examination to terrifying diagnoses, from ordinary burdens to extraordinary, we will bear them better if we bear them with and alongside our friends.

I do not know why, having witnessed this courage in many contexts, I continue to think of fortitude as powerful strength untainted by fear or vulnerability. We technically know this not to be true. Christians often quote God's words to Paul about the thorn in his flesh in his second letter to the Corinthians: "My grace is sufficient for you, for power is made perfect in weakness" (12:9). In the Middle English Bible, these words are translated, "And he said to me, My grace sufficeth to thee; forwhy virtue is perfectly made in infirmity."[33] Virtue *perfectly* made in infirmity, by God's loving grace. Strength in weakness. I am learning how to quit thinking of fortitude as strength in strength, or virtue in virtue. Instead, I imagine Christ's *tholing* in love at the start of this chapter. Cruciform fortitude is always a paradox.

At last, Lady Fortitude stands upon something rather curious: a winepress. As an image, this portrait of fortitude is static—but it promises more, beyond what we can see right now. The smallest trickle of wine emerges from the winepress. But there will be more. For Lady Fortitude stands upon it with her

---

33. Middle English translation of the Vulgate, *Wycliffe's Bible*, ed. Josiah Forshall and Frederic Madden (Oxford, UK: Oxford University Press, 1850).

heavy anvil and her cumbersome castle, slowly pressing the grapes into what will become, with time, a heady vintage.

Fortitude is a storybook virtue that we still love today (unlike meekness or abstinence, for instance). This storybook quality reveals something to us—the effects of fortitude are often hidden until the very end of the story. All the best heroes and heroines bravely bear much for the sake of love. I think of Anne Elliot, Frodo and Sam, Jo March. But we can't see how the wine flows from the winepresses until the story's end. This is true even in more ordinary stories than regency romances or Middle-earth journeys: *She joyfully taught hundreds of children how to read over many years of teaching; he is a recovering alcoholic now sober for decades; they were faithfully married for sixty years.* These stories are made up of a series of repeated, unseen-to-the-naked-eye decisions to be present to the need of the moment, to cleave to goodness as one is held in grace. And even then, all these labors of love are not quite the end of the story, for we often cannot see the full picture in this life.

This is also what the winepress reminds us. You stand atop the winepress now. But fortitude is never in vain. Fortitude is a practice of hope in the goodness of God. In this hope, we stretch toward the story's end beyond death. And though there is no wine fit to drink yet, there will be flagons and bowlfuls of it in the superabundance of Christ's table.

Practices and Prayer

> Keep alert; stand firm in the faith; be courageous; be strong. Let all that you do be done in love. (1 Cor. 16:13–14)

Practices

- Check in regularly on a friend who needs love right now. Text, call, send a joke, make dinner, choose to be intentionally present in another's need. Alternatively, ask a friend for this, if you need this right now. Sometimes it takes tremendous fortitude to confess a need for help.
- Reflect on these questions with a trusted friend, family member, or spouse:
  - *What are your present anvils? Where do you need strength in vulnerability right now?*
  - *What dragons—whether acts or thoughts or feelings—might you need to face in the fortitude of confession?*
- Read further on fortitude: *The Lord of the Rings* trilogy by J. R. R. Tolkien (so many different kinds of fortitude), *In This House of Brede* by Rumer Godden, *Team of Rivals* by Doris Kearns Goodwin.

Prayer

Lord Jesus, give me fortitude. Help me to face the most challenging and exhausting situations in my life with the determination to love well. Help me to bear my anvils [name them here]. Give me the courage to look at the dragons in my castle and pull them out, not to run away from them, but to confess them and make amends. Most of all, increase my hope in the work you are doing in the world. May I walk in that hope after you. Amen.

CHAPTER SIX

AVARICE AND MERCY: HEDGEHOG AND OLIVE OIL

Sow ye for yourselves rightfulness in truth, and reap ye in the mouth of mercy, and make ye new to you a field newly brought to fallow. For it is time to seek the Lord, and when he cometh, he shall rain blessings upon you.

—Hosea 10:12 (Middle English Bible)

The quality of mercy is not strained.
It droppeth as the gentle rain from heaven
Upon the place beneath. It is twice blessed:
It blesseth him that gives and him that takes.

—William Shakespeare

In a medieval prayer book now called *The Dunois Hours*, a personification of Avarice rides across the manuscript page.[1] Avarice is a vacant-eyed young man, almost unfocused around the edges, who holds a chest filled with gold. But Avarice and his gold pale in comparison to the creature he is astride: a massive monkey. The monkey looks frighteningly sharp and aware as it gazes directly at the viewer of the prayer book. Behind man and monkey, heaps of coins gleam unnoticed upon a table. Another man slightly off-frame carries a giant money bag and tries to hand it to absent-minded Avarice.

The illumination resembles a dreamscape, a world where everything is slightly off-kilter. Avarice's feet aren't visible. His robes part a little, only to reveal more fur. Is it the fur of his mantle or the fur of the monkey? Is he melting into the monkey? At any rate, Avarice is unperturbed. Defying our expectations, he ignores the man handing him more gold (shouldn't he be greedily grasping it?), continuing to stare absently at the casket in his lap.

Avarice seems to have a tenuous grasp on reality—which is exactly the point. Theft, miserliness, and hoarding money are all merely symptoms of something more severe and insidious. *Avarice has lost the ability to see true value.* Bad accounting (forgive me the pun).

Avarice is the capacious term for a whole host of disordered attitudes about money, material goods, and acquisition. Though we more frequently use the word *greed* today, *avarice* is broader

1. "Avarice," miniature in *The Dunois Hours*, manuscript illumination, ca. 1440–1450, Yates Thompson 3, fol. 174r, British Library, London, last updated May 23, 2018, https://commons.wikimedia.org/wiki/File:The_Dunois_Hours_Avarice.jpg.

"Avarice," miniature in *The Dunois Hours*, manuscript illumination, ca. 1440–1450, Yates Thompson 3, fol. 174r, British Library, London. From the British Library archive / Bridgeman Images

than *greed.*[2] Money is not evil per se; it can either help us or impede us in our vocation to love. Avaricious actions and attitudes include both hoarding and the burning desire to acquire, but they also include paired opposites like stinginess and extravagance, or particular actions like usury (lending with interest), simony (the selling of spiritual offices or sacraments), theft, and withholding. This cluster of behaviors and character qualities falls under the habit of valuing one's money or material goods higher than other lives around oneself. Avarice entails a growing and even cultivated blindness to the needs of others in pursuit of the glittering mirage of one's own material desires and goals. Because of this nurtured ignorance, avarice is a mother to injustice, corruption, slavery of all varieties, and systemic poverty.

In the Sermon on the Mount, Jesus's exposition on the shape of the life following him further up and further in to the kingdom of heaven, he describes the kinds of treasures we are called to gather:

> Do not store up for yourselves treasures on earth, where moths and vermin destroy, and where thieves break in and steal. But store up for yourselves treasures in heaven, where moths and vermin do not destroy, and where thieves do not break in and steal. For where your treasure is, there your heart will be also.
>
> The eye is the lamp of the body. If your eyes are healthy, your whole body will be full of light. But if your eyes are unhealthy, your whole body will be full of darkness. If then the light within you is darkness, how great is that darkness!
>
> No one can serve two masters. Either you will hate the one and love the other, or you will be devoted to the one and

2. For more on the development of avarice as a concept, see Richard Newhauser's *The Early History of Greed* (Cambridge University Press, 2000).

> despise the other. You cannot serve both God and money (Matt. 6:19–24 NIV).

Jesus's comment on quality of vision, sandwiched between considerations of attitudes toward money and material goods, almost seems like an aside. But it is not. Our relationships to money and material goods guide our ability to recognize true value, to evaluate well, to judge well.

Where your treasure is, there your heart will be also. If avarice is the self-inflicted bad reckoning of value, mercy is above all the habit of seeing the hidden treasure, the image of God, in other people, especially when such sight is difficult or nearly impossible. Mercy restores the rightful relationship between goods and people.

Why mercy and not the more expected antidotes to avarice, like generosity or liberality? Generosity and liberality, as giving beyond what is expected, are beautiful, much-needed virtues that should not be underestimated. They often appear in medieval writing as part of the array of antidotes to avaricious habits. But unmoored from mercy, generosity or liberality can participate in systems of patronage and giving that reinforce the hierarchies of the deserving and the undeserving. I give my hard-earned money to you because you have none (or, sometimes implicitly, *because you have failed/are lesser/can't do it*). Aren't I great? Aren't you grateful?

In contrast, mercy is a friend to those the world has learned to ignore: the guilty, the disabled, the sick, the weak, the sinners. In other words, every single person needs mercy. Mercy shatters the rigidity of judging value solely through earning and growth charts and good grades. It reveals in daylight the tawdry, false sheen of boot-straps success and narratives of self-making. Mercy belongs to redemptive reckoning as it allows one to recognize and value people in their truest identities beyond present circumstances of evil, indigence, or error—children of God, brothers and sisters in Christ, made for love itself. Mercy looks through the eyes of the crucified Jesus, who called out from the cross for divine mercy toward those torturing him while they were dividing his last earthly possessions (Luke 23:34). This true vision heals the plague of spiritual unseeing caused by avarice.

Becoming Beastly

The relationship between wrongful evaluation of goods and spiritual blindness is ironic because in our topsy-turvy world, money usually gives a person visibility and significance. Wealth and power go together like bread and butter. Even *The Dunois Hours* survives because it is a precious luxury item, richly illustrated and carefully kept for hundreds of years. The artifacts of the wealthy survive, while we barely know about the lives of the poor. The needs of wealthy nations are attended to, the desires of those with money seen and answered. Wealth does not bestow on us the inherent value we already possess as children of God, but it makes us and our desires visible in the world's hardscrabble, time-bound wrestle of desire and need. Our acquisition is rewarded because hoarding and collecting proffer a worldly visibility and power hard to reject.

Jacob's Well notes that the avaricious man or woman is like an otter, a fox, and a hedgehog. One could decorate a baby's room with such a cute bunch of forest critters (although that seems like a bad beginning for moral formation). In the medieval imagination, each of these animals illustrates a different form of avarice. *Jacob's Well* explains: The otter stockpiles fish that inevitably begin to stink and sicken the poor otter. The fox is a "deceivable beast" who "devoureth and slayeth" his neighbor in pursuit of his desires.[3] In the medieval bestiaries, the adorable hedgehog goes about with his "scharpe pryckys" to gather a great store of apples, excessively profiting off the hard work of others for his own enjoyment.[4] There are numerous charming medieval illuminations of the hedgehog with his apples collected on his spines, trundling back to his lair.

Charm aside, these comparisons remind the viewer how particular orientations toward goods can make us act like unreasoning animals. In our desire for objects, we forget people. This temptation is available to everyone, whether you have a lot of money or a little. Bad habits concerning money cause those distinctively human powers—rationality and good judgment—to unravel and communal vision to dim. Every exploitative system, from human trafficking to slavery to chronically underpaid workers manufacturing cheap goods for ravenous Western appetites overseas, grows out of a wrongful evaluation of money over lives. Humans have even wreaked ecological catastrophe in the throes of avaricious consumption. Think of fast-fashion clothing filling up landfills or large-scale mining causing the devastation of landscapes, animal habitats, and water supplies. On an individual level, a person can elevate their desire for the perfect vacation experience or outfit over caring how the service workers or clothing makers are treated in the process. In this instrumentalizing invisibility, avarice destroys community as it elevates the desires of one individual or a

3. *Jacob's Well: An English Treatise on the Cleansing of Man's Conscience*, ed. Arthur Brandeis (Oxford: Horace Hart, Printer, 1900), 117–18.

4. *Jacob's Well*, 118; see also *Book of Beasts: The Bestiary in the Medieval World*, ed. Elizabeth Morrison (J. Paul Getty Museum, 2019), 22, for an explanation of the fox up to his wily tricks in bestiaries with example illuminations; on the hedgehog, see Ann Payne, *Medieval Beasts* (New Amsterdam, 1990), 59.

very small group above the needs of the many and, in the process, teaches a false gospel that one is self-made. Examples abound: in lobbyists enticing politicians to act against the will of their constituents through massive campaign donations, in companies raking in billions while raising prices of food, in churches covering up abuse for fear of a lawsuit, in a billionaire living in a mansion while mere miles away ten people crash in a roach-ridden apartment.

If humans are "dependent rational animals," in the apt phrase of the moral philosopher Alasdair MacIntyre, following the understanding of Saint Thomas Aquinas and Aristotle, avarice causes us to lose our sense of reckoning and valuing other people—to become undiscerning beasts.[5] Our spiritual eyes become clouded as we lose our ability to weigh value beyond what we can grasp in our sweaty paws.

Money Matters

Does this mean that any extraneous possessions at all, outside of the basics, are bad? Should we all make a vow of poverty? Philosopher Fr. Andrew Pinsent notes this difficulty in discerning avarice: "One of the peculiarities of the relationship of money and virtue is that there are cases of heroic virtue under surprisingly diverse conditions of material wealth."[6] Pinsent gives examples ranging from Saint Francis of Assisi, a young aristocrat who cast aside *all* his wealth, to Saint Homobonus, patron saint of businesspeople, who did all kinds of good with his money in

5. From Alasdair MacIntyre, *Dependent Rational Animals* (Notre Dame: Notre Dame University Press, 1999).

6. Andrew Pinsent, "Avarice and Liberality," in *Virtues and Their Vices*, ed. Kevin Timpe and Craig A. Boyd (Oxford University Press, 2014), 163.

his small Italian town. If we hold too tightly to any one particular inflexible, universal rule about money, we tend to get into trouble. Think of the hypocritical religious leaders of Christ's day, tithing even the smallest portion of spices but unseeing of the needs of others (Luke 11:42).[7]

What matters more is *how* we make money and *what* we do with it. In the Middle Ages, controversies raged around the Dominican and Franciscan friars. They had vowed to live in voluntary poverty, subsisting on alms, unlike traditional professed religious like the Benedictines, who lived in monasteries off both donations and the land. Many theologians and writers, including William Langland, the poet of *Piers Plowman,* felt that this voluntary poverty actually made the friars *more* vulnerable to the sway of money, not less.[8] Wealthy laypeople would bribe wandering friars to give them light penance in exchange for their confessions. This is simony, the sin of selling spiritual goods such as spiritual positions of authority and even sacraments. To give someone "short shrift" means to listen to a truncated confession (shrift) and impose the lightest of penance in return, neither giving their vices the proper attention nor fostering the depth of contrition needed for real spiritual change and communal harmony. A steady income made bribes and the selling of the sacrament less appealing, thought Langland and many others. Money has tempted many in the church to participate in shady deals at the cost of human suffering.[9]

---

7. The "one particular rule" difficulty could be extended to most of our temptations in general—the American Prohibition, for instance, turned out disastrous.

8. The collapse of the church is partially caused by the grasping greed of the friars in *Piers Plowman* C.XXII.

9. See Eugene McCarraher, *The Enchantments of Mammon: How Capitalism Became the Religion of Modernity* (Cambridge, MA: Belknap Press, 2019), for a devastating account of the church's complicity and convenient looking the other way with money during the rise of capitalism, especially regarding chattel slavery and prosperity gospel themes.

The way you get your money matters. The ends never justify the means, even if these means are legally and socially acceptable. Some avaricious ways of gaining money are obvious: theft, lying, fraud, and extortion. But there are also actions that, while legal, may not be right. Usury is the lending of money at very high rates, or any rates at all. Theoretically, medieval people believed Christians were not supposed to loan each other money with interest at all. Christians were supposed to loan freely and be ready to forgive those loans if the person couldn't pay them back in a reasonable way. Yet as it often happens with money, Christians found ways around these prohibitions that led to creatively awful results. The ruling Christian nobles who constantly needed to borrow money to fund wars and lavish lifestyles encouraged lending at interest from wealthy Jewish people. According to this system, the Jews could lend at interest because it wasn't Christian-to-Christian lending. Not only did this practice disregard the spirit of the warnings against usury by exploiting a loophole, it inflamed violent animosity and anti-Semitic stereotypes that still exist today.[10]

These rules feel strange to us today. Modern systems of credit cards, student loans, payday lending, and most mortgages would all have been considered sinful or at least questionable practices for early and medieval Christians to partake in as the person or institution loaning the money.[11] Today we live in a very

---

10. King Edward I even used usury as justification for expelling the Jews from England in 1290. See Julie Mell, "The Discourse of Usury and the Emergence of the Stereotype of the Jewish Usurer in Medieval France," in *The Myth of the Jewish Moneylender* (Palgrave MacMillan, 2018).

11. There is a robust, ancient Christian argument, rooted in the Hebrew Scriptures, for the forgiveness of long-term debt like student loans—fascinating given some of our current debates.

different economic society than feudalism, but remembering medieval people's moral qualms and missteps concerning lending at interest could lead us as Christians to fruitful questions about the central place of usury in our own economic systems—and perhaps reform.

Furthermore, the penitential manuals tell us, your career or craft matters. Formation does not happen in a vacuum. The things we do day-to-day lastingly shape us as we seek means to live. Medieval people held entertainment jobs like jugglers, public buffoons (I'm not exactly sure what that entails; perhaps some of our current American politicians apply), and heralds-at-arms (announcers for tournaments). They fell under a category one medieval book on penance calls "wicked crafts."[12] Prostitution and pimping were also included.

We might not categorize, say, sports announcers as "wicked" anymore. But I understand this as a challenge to us in postmodernity to attend to how our professions form our character. Some medieval penitential manuals posed questions based on the type of profession someone practiced, questions meant to help them recall and fully confess their sins.[13] The temptations of a pastor will differ from the temptations of a software engineer, which will also differ from the temptations of a caregiver of young children. How can we balance our glorification and pursuit of higher paid professions, like stockbrokers, professional athletes, tech folks, and so on, with the dearth of socially essential but undervalued

---

12. *The Book of Vices and Virtues: A Fourteenth Century English Translation of the Somme Le Roi of Lorens d'Orleans*, ed. W. Nelson Francis (Oxford: Oxford University Press, 1998), 41.

13. One example is the *Memoriale presbiterorum*, an instruction manual for priests that includes confession questions for specific social statuses and vocations (many thanks to Jessica Ward for the reminder).

positions like teachers, nurses, and garbage collectors? Because the ways we seek and earn money may shape us more than we realize, we are called to examine them. When profit becomes the bottom line, one can become especially prone to the habit of seeing dollar signs instead of people.

The School of Avarice

That our hearts stay with our treasure, whatever that is, reminds us that the deadliest aspect of avarice is its idolatry. *You cannot serve both God and money*. In disordered habits and desires toward money and possessions, on a practical level, we trust in the salvation of worldly goods and money to protect us from the vagaries of the universe. Avarice whispers that God's love is not superabundant but a limited resource that must always be buttressed by goods in case of a divine abandonment.

This behavior can occur quite subtly. The more I buy clothes or books, my two favorite expenditures, the more ideas I get for what else I want. I didn't know I wanted them until I saw them, but want them I do. (This burgeoning desire is, of course, aided and abetted by retailers and algorithm writers.) One could respond, "Grace, surely you aren't accumulating clothes or books with the idea of securing yourself against the abandonment of God." Certainly not on a conscious level. But am I buying them to feel better about myself or the world in a tactic I know will not work in the long run and distracts me from what is actually wrong? Sadly, yes. And so my petty idolatry gets me entangled in and feeds large-scale exploitative and ecological problems. Avarice's tentacles creep everywhere.

"But I'm not Jeff Bezos!" I may protest. Ultimately, avarice entails a habit of broken valuation influenced by but independent of actual possession. Humans always attempt to simplify avarice to something legible via dollar signs: *I couldn't be avaricious because I drive a dented Honda strewn with cracker crumbs, while she drives an immaculate Range Rover.* Yet the Desert Father Saint John Cassian grimly writes that "just as the words of the Gospel declare that even those who are not soiled in body have committed adultery in their heart, it is also possible for those who are not weighed down by money to be condemned along with the avaricious for their disposition and attitude. For it was the opportunity to possess that they lacked, not the desire."[14]

Ouch. This is why the Desert Mothers and Fathers, who did not own much of anything other than tattered robes, could still confess to avarice. However, it is simultaneously true that the more goods and money one possesses, the more opportunities one has to develop a habitual dependence on them that exceeds gratitude, fulfillment of basic need, and desire for good use.

A fourteenth-century monk, Michael of Northgate, translated one penitential text from the French that he called the *Ayenbite of Inwyt*, or the *Bite of Conscience*. In it, he describes avarice as a "greate scole" where all study and learn excessive desire, great and small, religious or not.[15] Since Brother Michael's time, Western Christians have unabashedly become doctoral candidates in consumerism. For most of us, myself included, it is avarice that instructs our habits

14. John Cassian, *The Institutes of the Cenobia and the Remedies for the Eight Principal Vices* 7.22, trans. Boniface Ramsey, OP, Ancient Christian Writers 58 (Newman, 2000). Initially found in Rebecca Konyndyk DeYoung *Glittering Vices: A New Look at the Seven Deadly Sins and Their Remedies*, 2nd ed. (Grand Rapids: Brazos, 2020), 119.

15. *Dan Michel's Ayenbite of Inwit*, ed. Richard Morris (N. Trübner for the Early English Text Society, 1866), 34.

of discerning what we need from what we want in terms of money and material possessions. How are we to leave this school behind?

Misericordia

Mercy. I breathe the word in and out in prayer; it animates my lungs in the liturgy. But I do not use it much outside the context of prayer. The Latin word for mercy is *misericordia.* Split this Latin word in two and you get the roots of our related modern word *misery* (*miseria*) and the Latin word for heart (*cor*). Mercy entails the gift of one's heart being pierced, materially moved, by the suffering of another. "Blessed are those whose heart is made miserable by another's want," as the *Summa virtutum* rephrases both Saint Bernard of Clairvaux and the beatitude itself (Matt. 5:7).[16] In acts of mercy, humans participate in the character of God's grace as they respond swiftly to the needs of others regardless of their merit or deeds. Mercy truly opposes avarice in every sense: Instead of participating in the dehumanization of others (and ultimately oneself) via the elevation of money and goods over people, mercy recollects personhood even in the most abject circumstances.

Mercy is "true profit," says *The Book of Vices and Virtues,* "a rich stone and precious that were good to all things."[17] Mercy practices proper reckoning, true valuing, good accounting in the economy of the kingdom of heaven, where all are made in Christ's image and all needy cries are worthy of attentive action. We live in a society that too often accords value to people via dollar signs,

16. *Summa virtutum,* 246.
17. *Book,* 195.

efficiency, productivity. But mercy exuberantly tramples over the usual divisions of prosperity and poverty, efficiency and inefficiency, skilled and unskilled. We all need that radical leveler, the mercy of God. God "is so *large* to us," joyfully muses the *Book*, and human mercy is our own outpour of this divine, capacious largesse.[18] In the midst of that joy of giving and receiving, mercy also entails sacrifice—the pain of witnessing, holding, and when possible, alleviating another's suffering. Mercy rejects the cultivated unseeing of avarice in favor of painful sight, of recognizing a fellow sufferer when one would really rather not. Highly inconvenient, always inefficient, sometimes excruciating.

Practicing mercy does not mean your heart is continually breaking in agony. Some folks are, indeed, given a particular gift of tears and lament.[19] But becoming a merciful person—a person who habitually practices mercy—does include cultivating a sensitivity and readiness to be broken. Often, this sensitivity and readiness is as simple as the acknowledgment that the one offering mercy is just as broken as the one receiving. Henri Nouwen, the beloved twentieth-century Catholic writer, urges us to recognize and "befriend" our individual brokenness and then place it under the blessing of God, "just as intimate a part of our being as our chosenness and our blessedness."[20] Recognition of the mutuality of our brokenness facilitates mercy. If we continually flee acknowledgment of our own brokenness, we will almost certainly flee the need

18. *Book*, 193.

19. We don't talk about this gift today as much, but in the Middle Ages, many people understood themselves as having the gift of tears for the world, like Margery Kempe or Saint Catherine of Siena. Perhaps this gift of the Holy Spirit is something worth pursuing and thinking about again.

20. Henri Nouwen, *Life of the Beloved: Spiritual Living in a Secular World* (New York: Crossroad, 1992), 75–76.

of others. The merciless do not recognize the unfillable depths of their own need; the merciful feel it with every bone and welcome it as kinship with one another in the far deeper mercy of God.

Illuminating, Cooking, Anointing

One of my favorite explanations of mercy comes from a popular sermon collection by the fifteenth-century cleric John Mirk.[21] Christ's body is like an olive tree, he says. Just as an olive tree yields olives and from them olive oil, Christ freely offers mercy, his flowing blood, from his wounded body. And like mercy, oil was used for many purposes. In the ancient and medieval world, oil fueled lamps that lit the dark premodern night. Though people do not often use oil for lamps anymore, mercy still resembles that flickering light. From relief workers risking their lives in natural disasters, to volunteers writing prisoners on death row, to blood donations pouring into hospitals after a mass shooting, mercy fuels a small flame's rebellion against the darkest moments of human violence or natural disaster. The defiant light of such mercy is what Fred Rogers famously directed us toward when he told frightened children (and adults) to "look for the helpers" in times of crisis.[22]

Oil is also used in cooking. I often cover the bottom of a hot pan with olive oil, pouring in mushrooms or vegetables or meat. The oil not only flavors the whole dish, every piece of it, but ensures things do not stick. In baking, oil binds ingredients together and provides moisture, but when lightly applied to the

21. John Mirk, *Mirk's Festial*, ed. Theodor Erbe (Early English Text Society, 1905), 152.

22. From a television interview, "Fred Rogers: Look for the Helpers," posted April 15, 2013, https://www.youtube.com/watch?v=-LGHtc_D328.

bottom of the pan, it also allows you to share without hacking it to pieces. Oil unites and divides with ease, covering and binding and paradoxically dividing, flavoring as it goes. As in oil, so in mercy. As it covers, mercy also divides, making it easy to share one's hard work in the pot, to give with joy. It can even flavor each action in dealing with someone difficult.

And lastly, oil was used in two highly sacred moments: to anoint monarchs at coronations and to bless the body as a soul left its earthly pilgrimage. We see the parallels between the oil of coronation and mercy in what the *Summa virtutum* calls the five species of mercy: to give, to lend, to pardon, to show compassion, and to correct the errors of others privately and kindly.[23] Mercy characterizes real leadership and authority as it gives and lends without taking advantage of the power afforded by money and distinction. Mercy gently corrects and pardons, as a merciful king does, saving his people from the full force of the awful consequences of their own decisions when he can. And at last, far from the glory of kingship, mercy is the only human thing left to us in our pain as we die. Nothing material can lastingly comfort the dying in the end; only human compassion can, in the bathing of a brow, in soft words, in keeping watch.

Ghostly and Bodily: The Seven Works of Mercy

The most popular, nearly universal way of conceptualizing mercy in the Middle Ages came in a list of deeds rather than an image or metaphor. For mercy, even more than other virtues, is an orientation of the heart that *flows into action*. A habit of mercy must

23. *Summa virtutum*, 260–2.

be cultivated. It will not develop automatically. To encourage this attitude and orientation toward mercy, medieval preachers and theologians taught a list of seven bodily (or corporeal) works of mercy, often accompanied by a list of seven spiritual ("ghostly") acts of mercy (bodily on top, spiritual on bottom):

1. To feed the poor.
2. To clothe the poor and the naked.
3. To lend to the needy and forgive their debts.
4. To visit and tend to the sick.
5. To welcome strangers and wanderers.
6. To visit and comfort prisoners.
7. To bury the dead.

1. To give good counsel.
2. To teach good to those you have authority over.
3. To chastise fools and wrongdoers.
4. To comfort the sick in heart and those in despair.
5. To forgive those who have trespassed against you.
6. To bear with sinners and the afflicted, for who is not a sinner?
7. To pray for all God's children.[24]

Material and spiritual care for other humans combats the affliction of avarice as each action bids one person to attend to another, one who could easily be ignored. These lists included no caveats about the worthiness or innocence of those in need. Visit

24. This list comes from *The Book of Vices and Virtues*, 204–209, and my word choice is a loose translation of the Middle English there. The list itself is nearly universal and ubiquitous.

the prisoners and aid them, regardless of what they've done. Feed and clothe those who need help, whether they are your own beloved children in your kitchen or strangers in the chains of drug addiction. Receiving strangers could include having a conversation with someone you are politically opposed to, talking to someone you don't know at church, or welcoming immigrants. These two sets of seven are remarkably flexible and at the heart of imitating Jesus.

The acts of mercy, also sometimes called acts of charity, do not only help others in need. They change us in our souls. Acting this way reorients us toward freedom and love and generosity itself. In the logic of habit, which slowly carves the heart like a river carving rock, each act of mercy forms our desire to truly see others beyond the life circumstances of pain and want in which they find themselves. The seven works of mercy do not make one the powerful patron we would all secretly like to be thought of as. Rather, they remind us that we are all needy and beloved embodied souls. Everyone appears on this list of those needing help. We were all once thirsty and naked babies, wailing at our mothers' breasts. I have been a stranger in a strange land before. You may remember a time you were a prisoner or lonely or ill. And every one of us will die. Our shared need of mercy places the truth of each life in clear brightness: *Everything we have is a gift.* The heart-knowledge of one's desperate need for mercy unlocks the sealed doors and covered windows of avarice.

Mercy and Justice Inextricable

This ancient list of bodily works of mercy originally stems from Matthew 25:31–46, in Christ's story of the sheep and the goats on judgment day.[25] In a series of stories of what the kingdom of heaven is like, Christ begins his next story: "When the Son of Man comes in his glory . . ." As he sits on his throne over the world, he will divide the sheep and the goats. He explains that the sheep have fed him, clothed him, tended to him in his sickness and imprisonment. The goats did none of these things; they looked the other way. Both groups are shocked: *When did we ever do (or not do) those things for you?* And the Judge answers that when they did these things for anyone, they were caring for the Son of the Living God himself.

Justice has long been defined as the virtue that enables a person to render another person his due.[26] Justice asks, then acts on, what we owe to one another. We embodied, limited humans have long set justice and mercy at odds, as one being the virtue that punished and one being the virtue that omitted punishment.[27] But in Jesus Christ, these virtues are united, inextricable from one another. They are both virtues of judgment.

From the tail end of the Middle Ages, one stunning portrayal of the seven works of mercy illustrates the gospel words vividly. The anonymous "Master of Alkmaar" painted a series depicting each bodily work of mercy, which now dwells at the Rijksmuseum in Amsterdam.[28] The set of panels once hung in an almshouse, and then for another four centuries, a church, reminding wor-

---

25. Burying the dead is the only act that does not appear in Jesus's original words. It was added to the works of mercy later.

26. A paraphrase of Aquinas following Aristotle, *ST* II-II.58.1.r.

27. For more on this opposition and a general consideration of mercy and its tensions in historical Christian thought, see Alex Tuckness and John M. Parrish, *The Decline of Mercy in Public Life* (Cambridge, 2014), especially the introduction and ch. 3.

28. Master of Alkmaar, *The Seven Works of Mercy*, oil on wood, ca. 1504, Rijksmuseum, Amsterdam. See the detailed and helpful catalog entry on the artwork on the Rijksmuseum website, https://www.rijksmuseum.nl/en/collection/SK-A-2815/catalogue-entry, accessed March 29, 2024.

shipers of their call to practice mercy. Each panel portrays one of the seven acts. And in each panel, the painter has hidden in plain sight Christ himself.

In the first three scenes (and the fifth), Jesus is one of the crowd of late medieval Dutch folk, distinguished only by his traditional long hair and beard. In the first panel, he looks straight out from the frame into the viewer's eyes. *Do you see me?* Jesus is thirsty in the crowd of unwashed, unimportant families. The pattern continues: Jesus is hungry. Jesus needs clothes. In the fourth panel, burying the dead, we get a cosmic glimpse of Matthew 25. Christ reigns above, showing his wounds in the traditional posture of medieval judgment day art.[29] But unlike traditional doomsday art, there are no graves opening up below, as the funeral goes on undisturbed. In the last two panels, the Master of Alkmaar shows us what else happens as we walk through the acts of mercy. Jesus is still in the frame, but in these last two scenes, he comforts prisoners. He tends to the sick. Viewers, called to mercy, can see *who* one becomes through the habit of acts of mercy.

We become Jesus as we learn to actively care for one another in our need. He, the man whose heart was literally pierced in the love and forgiveness of his enemies, is the embodiment of *misericordia*. But as the central panel reminds us, Christ is also enfleshed justice. As the only fair Judge of the hearts of humankind, he sees true value in full. Justice and mercy, not opposed but united in the only real Judge.

Mercy ends up not as excessive giving or generosity or pity or even simple compassion. *Mercy is the nearest human practice to*

29. Check out the Judge chapter from *Jesus Through Medieval Eyes* for more on this idea in medieval artwork of judgment day.

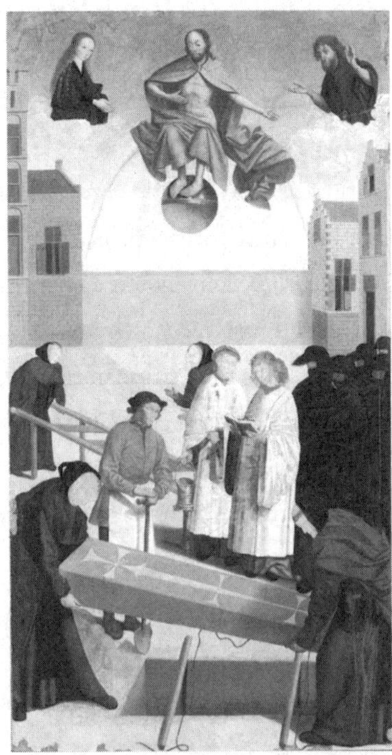

Master of Alkmaar, *The Seven Works of Mercy*, oil on wood, ca. 1504, Rijksmuseum, Amsterdam.

divine justice. Mercy is the closest equivalent to seeing how Jesus sees, to judging how Jesus judges, to loving how Jesus loves. It is rare for us to truly see what we owe to one another in our scattered blindness. But we can bear witness to our own mutual need and act on that in love. Mercy is the Christian's path into the perfect justice of God. With every act of mercy, my heart is pierced deeper and my eyes are opened wider to the presence of others—and the presence of Christ, in them, in me.

Practices and Prayer

> He hath shewed thee, O man, what is good; and what doth the LORD require of thee, but to do justly, and to love mercy, and to walk humbly with thy God? (Mic. 6:8 KJV)

Practices

- Reflect on these questions from two modern-day philosophers regarding your own use of money, and honestly share with a trusted friend, family member, or spouse:
  - *From Fr. Andrew Pinsent: Is your orientation toward money governed by human relationship?*[30]
  - *From Rebecca Konyndyk DeYoung: "If I keep handling possessions like this for the next ten or twenty years, what sort of character will I develop and what kind of person will I become?"*[31]

---

30. Pinsent, "Mercy and Avarice," *Virtues*, 172–4.
31. DeYoung, *Glittering Vices*, 114.

- Go out of your way to practice each of the seven bodily acts of mercy and the seven spiritual acts of mercy during a specific time period (the next month, Lent or Advent, over the next year). Some you might already do every day (caregivers to family members, I see you!), and some will be more elusive.
- Read further on mercy: *Just Mercy* by Bryan Stevenson, *Silas Marner* by George Eliot, *Piers Plowman* by William Langland (I recommend the translation by George Economou).

Prayer

Lord Jesus, make me merciful in body and soul. Have mercy on me, for I have ignored and hurt others by my acquisitive consumption. Detach my heart from the iron grip that my possessions have on me. Help me to use my money and material possessions wisely and well. Teach me how to spend, save, and give freely, guided by my relationships with my neighbor and creation. Give me your eyes, true vision, to see the image of God in every person I meet. Pierce my heart when I see need, and move me to act on that piercing so that I may follow you into true justice and mercy. Amen.

CHAPTER SEVEN

GLUTTONY AND ABSTINENCE: BEAR AND SONGBIRD

A grateful person offers praise
For all his Works and Ways,
And for the Glory which he sees
In the Bright Heavens above:
For all the Flowers and fruitful Trees
That do express his Love.
A blessed man is full of appetites,
And in the Glory of his God delights.

—Thomas Traherne

"Take, eat: this is my body."

—Mark 14:22 KJV

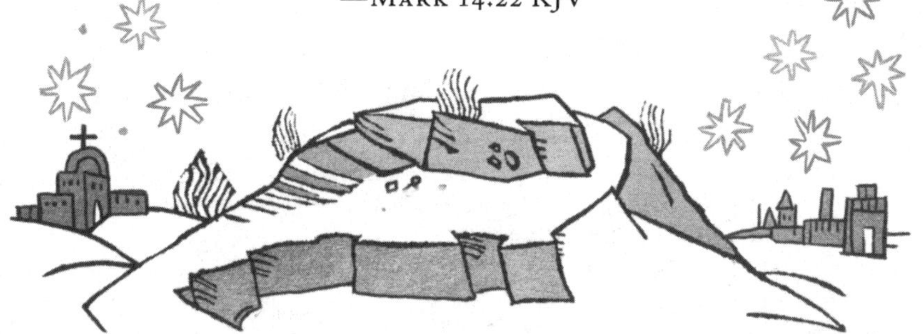

In William Langland's allegorical poem, *Piers Plowman,* we meet the seven capital vices as people on their way to confession. Glutton follows a circuitous path to his confession: He attempts to go to church, but the "hot spices" of the tavern allure him through its beckoning doors.[1] Inside, a motley company—Davy the ditcher, the Hangman of Tyburn, the clerk of the church, Cecily and Clement the cobblers, Godfrey the garlic-monger, and many more—argue, laugh, gamble, and most of all, consume to excess:

> Glutton had guzzled a gallon and a gill.
> His guts began to grumble as two greedy sows;
> He pissed a puddle the length of a pater-noster . . .
> (C.VI.397–9, translation mine)

Alas, the thought of peeing for the duration of the Lord's Prayer will live in my imagination until the end of my days. Glutton proceeds to get wasted with garlic-monger and company.

The next day, Glutton finally, groaningly makes it to shrift. The old guzzle-guts has a long list of sins to confess. But what draws together the long list of actions—as diverse as drinking before noon on a fast day to "sins of the tongue" like swearing—is that gluttony viciously shrinks the body into a tool for unbridled

1. Can you imagine what "hot spices" meant to a fourteenth-century English person? One of the spices on the list is "pepper." The level of food blandness must have been unbelievable. No wonder Glutton succumbed.

consumption and self-gratification. A fifteenth-century book to help discern vices in oneself says it well: "The sin is not in the meat, or drink, but in the appetite and desire thereof, when thy delight is out of measure therein."[2] In its measureless maw, the capital vice of gluttony masticates the communal and spiritual joys and complexities of eating into paltry self-pleasuring.

> Glutton ends with a pledge:
> For I vow to God himself, for any hunger or thirst,
> I won't even digest fish on a Friday in my belly
> Unless Abstinence my aunt has given me leave
> And yet I have hated her all my lifetime!
> (C.VI.425–441)

Glutton begrudgingly turns to the unwanted guidance of old "Aunt Abstinence" at the end of his confession—an idea that also fits our expectations. Abstinence definitely seems like a cantankerous crone embittered by her years of saying no to fun or tasty or easy things. Aunt Abstinence's strong modern association with the flickering fluorescent lights and gym smell of an American high school sex-ed classroom certainly doesn't help.

Thank goodness these impressions are quite wrong when it comes to abstinence as a real live virtue. Glutton bewails this virtue from the perspective of a Vice. Only a viciously incomplete understanding conceives of abstinence as a perpetual denial of the body's pleasures and needs. But what, then, *is* abstinence? Abstinence, sometimes called restraint, is the special variety of

2. *Jacob's Well: An English Treatise on the Cleansing of Man's Conscience*, ed. Arthur Brandeis (Oxford: Horace Hart, Printer, 1900), paraphrasing Saint Gregory the Great, 142.

the cardinal virtue of temperance that governs the manner of our eating. Sobriety is its sister virtue for drinking. And while both abstinence and sobriety share connotations of restriction, they are both virtues concerning the form and content of our desires, not complete negation. *The Book of Vices and Virtues* defines "sobrenesse" as "naught else but right measure," regarding eating and drinking but also attitudes toward food and drink and creation in general.[3] Abstinence and sobriety weigh how and what and where and what time we eat or drink, depending on the needs and invitations of the moment. As a habit of balanced care of the body's needs and desires regarding food and drink, these virtues are cousin to gratitude, hospitality, and justice. They reset us embodied, desiring creatures into our context, as beloved rational animals created for giving and receiving one another in our fullness.

Abstinence and sobriety (and their sister, chastity) are "species," to use the language of Saint Thomas Aquinas, of the cardinal virtue of temperance. Temperance, as the modern-day theologian Stanley Hauerwas put it, is "the virtue that shapes our wants."[4] The midcentury Thomist philosopher Josef Pieper renamed temperance "selfless self-love."[5] Loving the self and its desires does not always mean saying yes to it. It is deliciously ironic that temperance is the closest of all the remedy virtues to the occasionally dubious modern-day ideal of self-care. In our wealthy postmodern society, we focus more on what we give

3. *The Book of Vices and Virtues: A Fourteenth Century English Translation of the Somme Le Roi of Lorens d'Orleans*, ed. W. Nelson Francis (Oxford: Oxford University Press, 1998), 277.

4. Stanley Hauerwas, *The Character of Virtue: Letters to a Godson* (Eerdmans, 2018), 158.

5. Josef Pieper, *The Four Cardinal Virtues* (Notre Dame: Notre Dame University Press, 2014), 148.

ourselves—the "treat yourself!," the wish list, the fulfillment of desire. This is not always a bad thing. We must ask ourselves, then: When does full self-care, "selfless self-love," mean turning away from what we want in the moment? Where do balance and space rather than consumption inculcate individual and communal wholeness in our desires?

The Body and Its Desires

To think clearly about gluttony and the temperance virtues, we must take a moment to consider bodies and pleasure. When the seventeenth-century poet Thomas Traherne rhymes, "A blessed man is full of appetites, / And in the Glory of his God delights," he expresses reality.[6] A desire and need to eat and drink belong to humanity made in the image of God. Christians worship a God who is fully man and fully divine, not a God costumed in a skin suit. The incarnation tells us this, and I cannot emphasize it enough: *Bodies, including your own, are good, totally independent of their shape or abilities.* Christians have learned so from Mary, who fed God in her womb, from Christ, who turned water into wine and fed hungry crowds. As much as magpies, mountains, and monsoons, my body is a window into the character of God. And like all of God's creation, these bodies and their pleasures require care and attention.

Yes, the pleasures too are gifts from God. Pleasure in eating was a contested question for some medieval folks.[7] Some thought,

---

6. Thomas Traherne, *The Works of Thomas Traherne*, ed. Jan Ross (D.S. Brewer, 2005), 405.

7. See, for instance, *Jacob's Well*, 146.

to paraphrase Winnie the Pooh, savoring a smackerel wouldn't get you sent straight to hell, but it would earn you some years in purgatory as a venial sin. Thankfully, many theologians like Aquinas dismissed that view.[8] Many medieval people would be hesitant to follow this logic, but the pleasure from eating and drinking forms us in soul almost as much as the physical nourishment. One of my favorite questions to ask people is, "What are some of your favorite meals you've had?" Even briefly thinking of my own fills me with joy: 2005, California Pizza Kitchen in North Phoenix: barbecue chicken salad, six seventeen-year-old girls driving ourselves (!) on the first day of our senior year for lunch; 2015, early morning sun filtering onto a hospital bed in North Carolina: my favorite tea with cream and honey and a scone with copious clotted cream, my hours-old daughter in my mom's arms next to my dad and my husband. The pleasure of the food was wonderful. But the meals were especially wonderful (and even more delicious) because they were happening at moments when I was becoming more myself.[9]

Food is part of remembrance, healing, the building of social bonds. Feeding one another and eating together is an act of social significance. By cooking for you or buying you dinner, I recognize you as a fellow image-bearer. No wonder so many cultures ancient and modern have strict rules concerning hospitality and what humans owe to one another! The first chapter of John's gospel tells us the good news: God gives himself to us in Jesus

---

8. *ST* II-II.148.1.r. Aquinas clarifies that it is inordinate desire that gets you in trouble, not any desire for food and drink.

9. For more on the connections between food and identity, see Robert B. Kruschwitz, "Gluttony and Abstinence," *Virtues and Their Vices*, ed. Kevin Timpe and Craig A. Boyd (Oxford University Press, 2014), 143–5.

Christ, the Word made flesh. And Christ chooses to give himself to us, to heal our broken social bonds, in the sacrament of the Eucharist—an act of communal eating and hospitality.

Hating the body and its gifts goes beyond bad self-esteem: It is a heresy. Saint John Chrysostom (ca. 347–407) was a noted ascetic who sometimes took bodily mortification too far—not a voluptuous pleasure-seeker by any stretch of the imagination. His surname, which is actually a nickname, means "golden tongue," for he was famous for his preaching. One day, as he preached on the uniting of two bodies in marital sex, the crowd became a little uncomfortable, shifted in their seats, and tittered and blushed in shame and disapproval. Old Goldentongue became irritated. "You are all behaving like a bunch of heretics!" he scolded.[10]

Chrysostom referred to an actual heresy called Manichaeism (or its closely related cousin, Gnosticism). Manichaeans taught that bodies are bad, especially in their natural drives for food and sex. These physical desires must be surmounted in favor of a sheer spiritual existence. Manichaeism rejects the limitations and givenness of the body in favor of a supposed purity of the mind and soul. Such a belief views the incarnation as crude and scandalous. What Chrysostom angrily pointed out is that some versions of Christianity skate very near to this heresy.

Historically, gluttony and abstinence (and by abstinence, I mean its sister sobriety as well) have been a tricky pairing, frequently shifting in their shapes and expectations. At times, resistance to gluttony has taken a form close to bodily self-hatred and the attempt to escape its dirty, vulnerable needs by denying it entirely. I feel uneasy when I read of medieval women like Saint

10. I came across this story in Pieper, *Four Cardinal Virtues*, 154–6.

Catherine of Siena or Angela of Foligno or Marie of Oignies who refused to eat anything other than the Eucharist, destroying their physical health.[11] Or the famous and influential male clerics who practiced a vigorously self-punishing ascetism, like Saint Bernard of Clairvaux, Chrysostom himself, or Saint Gregory of Nyssa, who argued at one point that taste is "the mother of all vice."[12]

It's not just them. Semiheretical hatred of the body inevitably pops up to this day when Christians turn to talking about our bodies, our bellies, and our desires. Recall the barely hidden disgust of the body manifest in the "purity culture" of the 1990s and early aughts, or the bodily disdain implied in whatever punitive "cleanse" or diet that celebrities are trotting out online right now. Yet resurfacing Manichaeism does not mean we throw gluttony and abstinence (or lust and chastity) out, as outdated relics of a backward past. The individualistic belief that what the mouth, stomach, or sex organs do has no bearing on the heart and mind, as long as they're not "hurting someone else," is actually a Manichaean-adjacent attitude. I still reduce my body to an object or empty vessel irrelevant to the "more important" spiritual stuff. In this chapter (and the next on lust and chastity), we fight a conceptual war on two fronts—against gluttony as a vice and against gluttony's comrade in arms, hatred of our bodies. An attentive, measured love for the body belongs to a people who worship God-with-Us, the Word become Flesh, the Bread of Life who feeds us with himself. And this means that how, what, and when we eat and drink matter too.

---

11. Caroline Walker Bynum treats women like these with scholarly respect and nuance in her book *Holy Feast and Holy Fast: The Religious Significance of Food to Medieval Women* (University of California Press, 1987).

12. Quoted in Bynum, 38.

Getting to Know Glutton

Let's return to Langland's Glutton, whose confession ironically guides us through the deeper nuances of gluttony beyond overeating. After his "prayerful" urination and some drunken escapades, Glutton's wife and serving maid bear him to his bed. When he wakes, he confesses to Repentance, a priestlike figure:

> To thee, God, I, Glutton, confess myself guilty
> Of that I have trespassed with tongue, I cannot tell
> how often;
> Sworn "By God's soul and his sides!" and "So help
> me, God almighty!"
> There was no need, and I did many times falsely;
> And I oversupped at my supper and sometimes at
> lunch,
> More than my body could digest,
> And like a dog that eats grass so I began to vomit
> And spewed out what I could have given—I cannot
> speak for shame
> The villainy of my mouth and of my foul gullet—
> And fasting-days before noon I guzzled ale
> Out of reason, among buffoons to hear their filthy
> jokes.
> For this, good God, grant me forgiveness
> Of my wicked living in all my lifetime. (VI.425–
> 437, translation mine)

Langland's Glutton echoes descriptions of the vice in more priestly materials, just with more flair. Excess is obviously one key element of gluttony's "measurelessness": overeating, drinking to insensibility, or ironically (and unmentioned by Glutton), restricting your intake because of stinginess or punitive dieting—refusing to eat when your body really does need food. Initially, this might look like gluttony's opposite, but it *ignores* the needs of the body to an excess. Gluttony's desire beyond measure also implicates extreme fastidiousness—being really picky or demanding, or eating only the most expensive or rich food.[13] Glutton also confesses to eating and drinking out of time or out of reason, like eating out of boredom when you're full or drinking in the morning.[14] Part of the "measureless" aspect of gluttony is the attitude best expressed by "I want it when I want it where I want it." Time, place, other people, and even the real needs of one's own body become subject to the tyranny of whim.

Medieval writers frequently compared gluttony to a pig, a familiar image, who will rummage in garbage to satisfy its unlimited appetite. However, a different animal also appears regularly. Great bearded Gluttony rides upon a large bear on his way to war in *The Assembly of Gods.*[15] The Carmelite friar Lavynham explains that the bear has such a great delight in honey that it will pursue swarms of bees back to their hive. These bees have

---

13. Every penitential manual mentions this, for one example, see *Jacob's Well*, 144. Of course, this does not include folks with dietary restrictions for health, disability, or in illness!

14. Our modern discoveries regarding addiction do not map neatly onto medieval ideas about alcohol consumption. It is important to recognize alcoholism as a disease. But this recognition is not mutually exclusive with the idea that there are ways of drinking—inside or outside alcoholism—that belong to a damaging, habituated practice.

15. *The Assembly of Gods: Le Assemble de Dyeus, or Banquet of Gods and Goddesses, with the Discourse of Reason and Sensuality*, ed. Jane Chance (Kalamazoo, MI: Medieval Institute Publications, 1999), ll. 628–629.

"travailed about" their honey for so long, but in minutes, the lumbering bear has licked their delicate labor entirely away.[16]

The gluttonous bear points us toward problems with measurelessness that go beyond our own bodies. Individual gluttony can prevent good care of creation and our care of other people. When desire and whim are the only measures for how and what I eat, I can easily ignore the fact that food is a gift and a finite resource and that how and what I eat affects ecosystems and communities other than my own.[17]

Gluttony was taken so seriously by medieval and patristic thinkers because they were able to recognize the far-reaching costs of this vice in ways that we in modernity, especially city dwellers like me, can often miss. In the Middle Ages, a bad harvest or lack of workers or death among sick animals had immediate and obvious impact. In today's globalized West, the struggles of the farmer, the impact of the weather, the hunger of our neighbor, the horrific treatment of the animals raised for food, and the widespread problems with pesticides are often hidden by our complex food systems. Yet these issues are still real. When we consume thoughtlessly, we can easily become numbed to anything but our own cravings. Gluttony demotes all bodies and food into vehicles on a pleasure ride. Meeting the needs of the body, forging community, and caring for the creation that feeds me all are pushed aside. Whose labor, or livelihood, or habitat do I sometimes lick away in unconsidered pursuit of my own pleasure?

---

16. Richard Lavynham, *A Litil Tretys*, ed. J. P. W. M. van Zutphen (Rome: Institutum Carmelitanum, 1956), ll. 21–26.

17. See Norman Wirzba, *Food & Faith: A Theology of Eating* (Cambridge University Press, 2011), for a thoughtful theological reflection on our distance from creation in how we often eat in western culture.

A Parody of Community

Gluttony's reductive nature threatens the possibility of real, embodied fellowship among God's creatures. Eating and drinking habits extend into a social and spiritual dimension. There's a category of gluttony that the penitential manuals dwell on at length: "sins of the tavern," which adds sins caused by drunkenness, like lechery and assault.[18] The *Book of Vices and Virtues* uses a favored metaphor when it describes the tavern as "the devil's chapel," where the devil performs his "miracles" among his acolytes and worshipers. Instead of the miracles of God seen at shrines and cathedrals, like the blind seeing and the paralyzed walking, "the devil does the contrary of all this in the tavern. For when a glutton goes to the tavern he goes with easy haste, but when he comes out he lacks a foot that will bear him, and when he goes thither he hears and sees and speaks and understands, when he comes thence all these abilities have been lost."[19]

This exemplum amusingly sounds like the kind of lecture an anxious parent would give their college kid about drinking. However, it gestures to a deeper undermining of community itself.

Medieval Christians believed, as many Christians still do, that the Eucharist, as an act of communal eating, is God's physical, direct sharing of himself and his love. In sharing drinks or a meal, we create mutual, sacrificial fellowship by divine design. Extreme or repeated drunkenness and all the behaviors around it create a simulacrum of real intimacy, real joy. This also explains why gluttony featured another, similar category called "sins of the mouth."

18. For example, *The Book of Vices and Virtues*, 53–54.

19. *Book*, 53–54, my translation.

Glutton first confesses to having "trespassed with tongue." He isn't referring to his eating but to the way that he speaks. As *The Book of Vices and Virtues* comments, "The mouth has two offices, that serveth to the swallowing of meat and drink, or that serveth to speech."[20] Idle talk, foul jokes, boasting, contempt, false modesty, flattery, perjury, chiding, murmuration, and blasphemy all fall under gluttony.[21] These self-gratifying modes of speech undermine and destroy community, either through direct conflict (contempt, perjury, chiding) or creating a false camaraderie that only stymies real connection or builds such connection on the tearing down of others (flattery, boasting, false modesty, "locker room" talk). We live in a gluttonous culture in more ways than one. Under the banner of "free speech," in doomscrolling or anonymity online, in mockery or in devouring of cable news, we can talk or consume others' talk gluttonously, speaking only out of our own pleasures and desires, uncaring—even gleeful—in how our words destroy the possibility of communion. May we Christians not confuse the real good of political freedom of speech with the viciousness of heedless, measureless language.

Gluttony offers a hypocritical imitation of both fellowship and loving the body. Repeated, measureless consumption, whether in food, drink, or speech, ends up in the same place: more craving, less real satisfaction and communion. Though gluttony focuses on food and the community of the body, unconsidered, *possessive* pursuit of knowledge or beauty or any pleasurable gift works the same, as we will see in the following chapter on lust

20. *Book*, 46.

21. You have seen them before—they occur with other capital vices too, like envy and pride. To riff off John Donne, no vice is an island. They are deeply interconnected, as in that appropriate medieval emblem of vices and virtues as limbs of a tree.

and chastity. It's the final twist in the irony of gluttony—in the unrestrained pursuit of pleasure, pleasure ceases to satiate.

The Gift of Context

While writing this chapter, I went on a long walk one afternoon, hoping to untangle some gnarled threads in my mind. It was the first spring day with the hints of summer in it. On my way home I passed five teenage girls walking toward the creek.

The girls were walking in the narrow path two abreast, laden with fat books. The last was carefully bearing a giant sepia-toned pitcher of lemonade, the kind that has been in your grandmother's kitchen since the 1980s. They had been laughing and chatting among themselves, but they fell silent as I approached, and I was struck by a strange beauty. The joyful, quiet girls in a line reminded me of a procession, nearly sacramental in its serious pursuit of embodied joy. The lemonade in its ugly pitcher might as well have been the sacrament itself. The warm spring air, the sunshine, the song of the water and birds, the words of friends and books, the tart lemonade—none of these gifts were to go unnoticed, unappreciated, unloved. I felt foolish, but I cried a little afterward, recollecting the moment, for I felt it was a vision of temperance in its fullness.

The ends of eating and drinking are physical and spiritual nourishment in the context of the gift of creation, especially food and bodies. If gluttony diminishes these gifts into pursuit of pleasure, temperance, in particular abstinence and sobriety, measure and give space for that spiritual and physical nourishment to happen in real fullness.

A feast day, like that the girls with the lemonade pitcher and books were celebrating, or a fast day, for that matter, always dovetail to deeper reality. Bodies do not float in a void; they always have a place, a time, a purpose. Occasions for eating, like funerals and birthdays, inherently contextualize a life, a body. A day like today was made for a pitcher of lemonade and companionable reading in deep enjoyment of the bodily gifts of God. Not in opposition but in complement: A day like today calls for fasting and prayer and silence, for taking the space needed to reset everything in context. Part of the work of temperance as a whole and abstinence in particular is to recognize our own bodies in the rhythms of created time and space.

For the pleasure, the real joy, comes not with consumption and excess but with the space we give one another, the thought and care given to setting, food, and companions. We have all been to parties *not* like this—where the host dominates or the guests are ungrateful, where the food is inadequate or bad, where discord looms. Temperance in its form of abstinence (and sobriety) sets the table or carries the lemonade, puts out the flowers, the silverware, invites the guests, eats thoughtfully and with relish and gratitude. The virtue does not entail a great denial of the gifts of the body, but enjoyment of them in the time and place given to us.

Abstinence's name may mislead us, for it does not merely consist in saying no or abstaining. Fasting is a significant part of abstinence, but not all of it. The medieval Franciscan Saint Bonaventure (ca. 1221–1274) reminds us that abstinence is an inward habit:

> The virtue of abstinence is in two parts. One is within, in the mind; the other without, in behavior. And that which is in the mind is to be observed always, but that which is in behavior is

> to be displayed according to circumstances. Indeed John, who was a pure man, practiced abstinence as much in mind as in body in order that he not be despised; but Jesus, who is truly our humanity, who was incapable of sin, used food and drink for a time. . . . Nor should you believe in any way that it is a greater virtue to abstain from food than to make use of food in moderation.[22]

Set in this light, practices of abstinence include the obvious (fasting in prayer, eating for physical nourishment) but also hospitality and good manners, following the liturgical year's cycle of fasting *and* feasting, and gratitude. I would also add, from a modern perspective: eating well according to the needs and love of creation. These abstinent practices entail more than saying no, but in their fullness necessarily curb bottomless and selfish desire. Hospitality and good manners require thought and action beyond personal convenience. Following the liturgical year means that sometimes I will feast and sometimes I will fast (and not necessarily from food).

Abstinence so often emphasizes constraint because saying no to one's various appetites is notoriously more difficult, perhaps at times impossible, than taking what one wants. Everyone finds it disagreeable to say no to food or media or something we want to say, when we *could* eat it, have it, do it. As an American, from my youth I have been trained to want, and to take, and to say yes to the minutiae of passing bodily desires. From the ubiquity of advertising to the enormous selection at the supermarket,

22. Bonaventure, *Vitis Mystica*, additamentum 5, chap. 42, par. 135, *Opera omnia*, vol. 8 (Quaracchi: Collegium S. Bonaventurae, 1898), 216–17, trans. Bynum, *Holy Feast*, 43.

one's desires are consulted and considered and honed almost each moment of the day. This is not always a bad thing, but it can control us, like Pavlov's dog. Saying no when I could say yes feels like swimming against a strong current. But the pause frees me to question the desires themselves. What is good, truthful, and life-giving in them? What is not?

Learning to Listen

Medieval writers tell us that abstinence resembles a whole-body *listening*. "We have only one mouth but two ears," *The Book of Vices and Virtues* reminds us.[23] In other words, talking is necessary, and how doubly necessary listening is to a life of wholeness and communion! Listening and silence are not lacunae but real actions. True fellowship would not exist without our ability to silently take in another's thoughts, to temporarily submit our own to theirs, to pause, to understand, to respond. Without choosing silence, we would be left talking over one another, creating a mumbling mess of missed connection. A fully abstinent life looks like a conversation. Out of the dance of speech and silence, pauses between words, pauses between bites, we respect and obey; we savor and listen and grow. *Measure.*

As abstinence listens to and obeys the needs and limits of the body, it also listens to and obeys the needs and limits of creation. In modernity, this means Christians should carefully consider how we consume and eat in relation to creation and its limits. Should I begin a practice of fasting? Buy local food at a higher

23. *Book*, 277.

cost and get fewer fun snacks as a result? Grow some of my own food? Monitor some of the other things I consume, like media or music or news?[24] These are actually Christian questions, questions of abstinence. In asking them and listening, one begins to listen to and obey the Lord of creation.

This good, discerning listening to the body, creation, and thus the Lord naturally draws us into the measure of time and place. Sometimes you eat and drink together in community. Sometimes you fast and pray alone. Sometimes with great joy you eat expensive sushi on your birthday or imbibe the best wine at a wedding. But eating with rich extravagance every day would not be good for your body or your soul, and no one should ever drive drunk. Temperance discerns and acts on the needs and invitations of the moment. Measure, *The Book of Vices and Virtues* tells us, comes not only in how we eat and drink but in all the workings of the will and its desires: in our faith, in our desires for the good gifts of God, in speech and clothing and bearing.[25]

Fasting like a Songbird

Fasting from food has always been the main historical practice to foster the virtues of temperance. Perhaps fasting makes you think of a sour-faced fellow churchgoer or of wild-eyed hermits in the Egyptian desert. But I am learning instead to think of the

---

24. These are the questions for my own context, a healthy, middle-class, city-dwelling American. Abstinence questions might be very different for you. A single mom debating how she will feed her children or a chronically ill person will have different questions about how to honor creation and bodies.

25. *Book*, 277.

white-crowned sparrows, house finches, and mourning doves outside the window in early dawn. Songbirds sing with joy in the morning, filling the light-streaky sky with praise before they eat, teaches the *Summa virtutum*.[26] These songbirds are examples of fasting. Fasting is more than just not eating for a period of time. That same sermon collection reminds readers of the ancient dictum that "the withdrawal of food is not meritorious unless it is done voluntarily out of love."[27] Fasting should not be a dour rehearsal but an intentionally cheerful, ordinary practice (Matt. 6:16–17).

Fasting is not inherently virtuous. In fact, medieval writers are careful to note that fasting for wrong reasons (excessively, or for spiritual points) offers its own set of temptations. "God wants to be served prudently, not that his servants should grow weak through excessive abstinence and then have to seek help from the doctors. Moderation is in order," preaches Saint Ambrose.[28] Saint Bernard cautions against fasting in a proud desire to be spiritually exceptional, like the Pharisee in Luke 18:9–14.[29]

Fasting is not for everyone, nor is it a necessary practice of holiness.[30] Our forefathers and foremothers in the faith carefully instructed pregnant and nursing mothers, the ill, the young, and the elderly against fasting. Fasting as a virtuous practice is done only out of love, which includes a love for the body and for one another. If a person fasts when her body really needs food—pregnancy, illness, frailty—then it cannot be done out of love. If a person has struggled with an eating disorder or suffers under

26. *Summa virtutum*, 268.
27. *Summa virtutum*, 266.
28. Qtd. in *Summa virtutum*, 274
29. Qtd. in *Summa virtutum*, 276
30. *ST* II-II.147.4.sed contra.

chronic illness, fasting from food is likely not a practice of love but an impediment to loving God, oneself, and neighbor well. However, those who should not fast from food can practice abstinence in other ways. You can fast from hatred or, in our modern context, certain forms of media or communication.[31] Fasting people were often encouraged to give the food they would have eaten to people who really needed it.[32] If you cannot or should not fast from food, intentionally sharing food with others is a beautiful and traditional way to participate in the spirit of fasting.

But why fast from anything at all? Fasting, comments *Summa virtutum*, drawing on a whole slew of ancient ideas, is good for a healthy body and soul. It "tames our flesh," "strengthens our spirit," "conquers the vices," "helps our prayer," and "disposes our soul to receive the Holy Spirit."[33] The first three reasons go hand in hand. In a society where food scarcity was common, to give up food or types of food for a time was not a small inconvenience. It was often seen as the greatest trial for temptation.[34] Medieval preachers often compared fasting to a horse's bridle, which allows the rider to steer the horse on a journey or stop entirely.[35] If one can withstand the sharp pangs of hunger for a short time, one can begin to withstand other desires, like lust or greed, that may be hurtful and damaging to ourselves and our neighbors. Fasting helps one to move beyond acting on impulse into acting with intention.

---

31. A medieval commonplace, for instance, *Fasciculus morum*, 61.

32. "Let the abstinence of the faithful become the nourishment of the poor and let the indigent receive that which others give up," Pope Leo the Great, Sermon 20, Ninth Sermon for the December Fast, pars 2–3, PL 54, cols. 189–90, trans. in Bynum, *Holy Feast*, 31.

33. *Summa virtutum*, 274.

34. Bynum, *Holy Feast*, 33–47, for changing attitudes on fasting and temptation.

35. *Book*, 281.

The latter two reasons, aid in prayer and the disposition of the soul for grace, are also tied together. Abundance of food at all times, like abundance of money or cleverness or beauty, can sometimes cause us to lose sight of our true dependence on God, one another, and the gifts of creation. When we voluntarily abstain from food or other gifts for a time, we recollect who we are beyond the facade of achievement and desire. We are beloved creatures of dust made in the image of God. This identity is not contingent on outward circumstances, neither personal successes nor failures, neither times of material prosperity nor times of long, dry thirst.

The Book of Vices and Virtues says abstinence resembles a person sitting and resting on the edge of a green well and looking down at the still water. You see your own image reflected below, which is in the image of the Creator: "The heart knoweth himself ther-in and seeth his creator, right as a man may see himself in a fair well."[36] When I remember who I am and who God is in the still waters of listening and fasting, I am more ready to recognize and receive whatever subtle or surprising grace comes, however it comes.

The historical church has given a great gift to help us practice temperance and recollect ourselves: the liturgical year. After the darkness of Good Friday and the silence of Holy Saturday arrives the light and song of Easter; after the trembling waiting and longing of Advent comes the fullness of Christmas. Traditionally, the Easter and Christmas seasons last more than a day too, to match the lengthy fasts before. In this ancient cycle of fasting *and* feasting, we learn how to see ourselves as more than consumers frantically squeezing the juice out of the lemon until it dries up.

---

36. *Book*, 278.

As theologian Joan Chittister writes, "Natural time requires us to think of ourselves as moving from energy to decay. This is a life bounded by years of toil, years of diminishment, a movement from more physical life to less physical life. Liturgical time . . . enables us to see ourselves moving from spiritual emptiness to spiritual fulfillment, from less of one dimension of life to more of another deeper, more meaningful kind of life."[37]

We are our beautiful bodies—and more than our bodies too. In fasting, we undergo minideaths; in feasting we taste the perilous joy of full life. Together, they deepen rather than diminish the quality of our desires. We relearn ourselves as spiritual embodied creatures.

Carpe Diem, Fellow Pilgrims

Fasting, the church calendar, and practices of abstinence all remind me of my human needs, and all remind me of my death too. As it turns out, both gluttony and abstinence are directed by ever-present human uncertainty about the ends of bodies and concern opposing notions of *carpe diem*. Gluttony follows the fearful suspicion that life is passing us by, so we devour what and while we can. Pleasure is fleeting. Death is coming. In a bonus, gluttony anesthetizes one against thinking too much about these endings.

Abstinence agrees: Seize the day, yes. But what kind of day is it? Where are its joys and demands? What does the gift of this

37. Joan Chittister, *The Liturgical Year: The Spiraling Adventure of the Spiritual Life* (Thomas Nelson, 2009), 40.

day ask of me? What is it offering to me? Abstinence and discernment are wrapped up together, and the shape of the present (in a double sense) looks wildly different in each individual life. But implicit in these questions is the faith that there will be abundance, in the end. I can say no now for the love of my body and soul and my neighbor and creation because the end is always a *yes, yes, yes.*

We are not slowly disintegrating people stumbling into increasingly enfeebled pleasures until the party's over. We are pilgrims on the spiraling path where we are reborn, learn, die in small ways, stumble again, receive—all the way held in mercy, all the way into bodily resurrection (1 Pet. 2:10–12).

Practices and Prayer

> And you, employing all care, minister in your faith, virtue; and in virtue, knowledge; And in knowledge, abstinence; and in abstinence, patience; and in patience, godliness; And in godliness, love of brotherhood; and in love of brotherhood, charity. For if these things be with you and abound, they will make you to be neither empty nor unfruitful in the knowledge of our Lord Jesus Christ. (2 Pet. 1:5–8 DRA)

Practices

- Pick a morning or day of the week to fast from food or something else you use or think about daily. The traditional days are Wednesday or Friday, if you'd like to fast with the companionship of the historical church, but you could pick any day for this kind of reflective intentionality regarding the gifts of the body.

- Reflect on this question and honestly share with a trusted friend, family member, or spouse: What does my particular context (place, work, family, age, health) direct me toward in beginning habits of eating and drinking that glorify God and respect his creation?
- Invite someone over for dinner or dessert. Cook for them if you can. Listen well. Let go of perfection and enjoy the time together.
- Read and watch further on temperance: read Norman Wirzba's *Food and Faith*; L. M. Montgomery's *Anne of Green Gables* books, which take such joy in parties, eating, and creation; or watch *Of Gods and Men* (one of the most profound feast scenes I've ever seen).

Prayer

Lord Jesus, make me temperate in my body and soul. Forgive me for the ways in which I have diminished my body and the gifts of creation into tools for my pleasure. Thank you for giving me the gift of pleasure while eating, and the joy of communion in feasting. Teach me how to say no when I should, to leave room, to cultivate silence in the conversation of life together. I am truly thankful for the delicious gifts you give me. Give me a vision of how to care for creation and my neighbor well as I eat in my particular setting. Let me rejoice in my bodily limitations as I walk the spiraling path towards eternal life. Amen.

CHAPTER EIGHT

LUST AND CHASTITY: CLOWN AND UNICORN

Virtue is not the absence of vices or the avoidance of moral dangers; virtue is a vivid and separate thing, like pain or a particular smell . . . Chastity does not mean abstention from sexual wrong; it means something flaming, like Joan of Arc.

—G. K. Chesterton

Love is the fulfilling of the law.

—Romans 13:10

A woman, hair unbound and flowing down her back in representation of her virginity, stands with her handmaiden in a hidden garden. They listen to the birdsong and rustling leaves. She waits for a unicorn, whom only she can catch and tame—long enough, at least, for hidden hunters to kill it and obtain its magical horn, which will heal any poison known to humanity. Otherwise, the beautiful and nervous creature would gore such hunters at first sight.

This scene takes place time and time again, in medieval bestiaries, in jewellike tapestries, in crumbling frescoes. Perhaps you yourself have seen the famously beautiful Hunt of the Unicorn tapestries at the Cloisters in New York City. In the Cloisters' tapestry, now damaged, we see only the gentle, elusive hands of the woman who has drawn the unicorn to herself.

Unicorns have long symbolized the virtue of chastity.[1] What is chastity, though? As one friend said to me with a sly grimace, "Isn't the chastity belt a medieval thing? That's the only thing I associate it with."[2] Alternatively, many people use it as a synonym for *virginity*, but everyone, regardless of their sexual experience, is invited into chastity. Saint Thomas Aquinas defines chastity as the habit of making "venereal pleasure," as he calls it, subject to

1. For more on unicorns, the Hunt of the Unicorn, and its connection to chastity in various artworks (including pictures of narwhal horns, which medieval people believed to belong to a unicorn!), see *Book of Beasts: The Bestiary in the Medieval World*, ed. Elizabeth Morrison (J. Paul Getty Museum, 2019), 3–4, 181, 194–97.

2. I happily repudiate its existence. See the very informative Katherine Harvey, *Fires of Lust: Sex in the Middle Ages* (Reaktion, 2021), 9.

one's reason.[3] As much as I love Saint Thomas (and agree with him), we are too enmeshed in the post-Enlightenment associations of reason with cold hard logic to make this a workable definition for us without scholastic study on the nature of reason. Who can think of sex in these terms without reducing a profound gift of God and a mystery to something calculated and disembodied?[4] Stick a pin in it then; let us return momentarily, for lust is far easier to understand.

Lust entails disordered sexual desire: inordinate, for the wrong person, at the wrong place or time, obsessive or possessive, or sexual habits ordered toward power or pleasure alone. These behaviors boil down to a core: In lust, one person uses another person for one's own pleasure and fulfilment of desire. It does not necessarily have direct relationship to the presence or absence of the sex act. Medieval English folk usually called it lechery. Like gluttony, lust functions reductively, shrinking down the complexity of another person into an object for pleasure. As with avarice, lust's acquisitive orientation toward other people disengages the lustful one from reality. In lust, no one is safe from using or being used—even if the sex is consensual, even if the sex takes place within marriage, even if no sexual act even happens.

That makes the unicorn hunt as a symbol of chastity rather ironic. For the unicorn is hunted in order to be used; the maiden's virginity is merely a lure for the slaughter of the great beast

---

3. *ST* II-II.151.5.r.

4. This is absolutely not how Thomas means it, but our language around reason is too diverging to pursue this thread helpfully without spending several pages trying to get to the bottom of things. For more on how Thomas understands reason more broadly, see Frederick Bauerschmidt, *Thomas Aquinas: Faith, Reason, and Following Christ* (Oxford University Press, 2015), especially Part I, "Faith and Reason"; for chastity, lust, and reason, Josef Pieper, *The Four Cardinal Virtues* (Notre Dame: Notre Dame University Press, 2014), 155–60.

and the use of its magical powers. Exceptionally ironic, given that postmodern Christians and non-Christians alike tend to teach that good sexual behavior leads to individual rewards. Whether we grow up conservative or liberal on sexual matters, we are taught that by behaving well sexually, a vibrant, fulfilling, and guilt-free sex life surely awaits us. By waiting to have sex until marriage, I will receive a completely healthy, pleasurable, and pure marriage. Or by having fully consensual sex with as many or few partners as I like, I will enjoy the fullest pleasure as well as the fullest possible version of my bodily freedom as an individual. We dangle carrots and strategically position maidenly laps in front of that sexy unicorn, hoping that by capturing it and claiming its power we can wield its magic for ourselves. Neither narrative is medieval.[5] The problem is that neither modern narrative nor, in many cases, the medieval one actually addresses the virtue of chastity, nor the root problems of lust.

Thankfully, a better unicorn hunt narrative of chastity exists: a tapestry of the annunciation in Ebstorf, Germany. Try in vain, you will never be able to recall a unicorn in the first chapter of the gospel of Luke, when the Angel Gabriel comes to Mary to announce that she will bear God in her womb. But this representation is symbolic: Mary sits on the ground in an enclosed garden. A small unicorn flees from graceful Gabriel behind him. The angel holds the leashes of hounds and blows a horn. These hunting dogs have names: Mercy, Peace, Justice. For God's mercy and justice are always at the bottom of incarnation, "chasing"

5. Medieval people vastly preferred complete and total sexual abstinence in virginity, which came with a special reward in the kingdom of heaven. Saint Thomas is representative: *ST* II-II.152.4 argues that virginity is the highest form of chastity and superior to chaste marriage.

God willingly into human flesh.[6] As the unicorn leaps into our mother's arms, she offers it space within herself. And Christ the unicorn comes to rest in the womb of the most chaste maiden who will bear him into the world. He alone heals the poison of sin, and he comes to willingly give himself in loving sacrifice.

Annunciation as the Hunt of the Unicorn, lectern hanging, ca. late fifteenth century, Kloster Ebstorf, Germany.
The Picture Art Collection / Alamy Stock Photo

In the annunciation tapestry, holy Mary and Christ himself both witness to the true nature of chastity. Mary's chastity does not originally come from her virginity. She is chaste in the deepest sense, in her *yes* to serving God with her whole heart and body. While vowed virginity has long been a radiant calling into chastity, and should be embraced again in our present

---

6. *Annunciation as the Hunt of the Unicorn*, lectern hanging, ca. late fifteenth century, Kloster Ebstorf, Germany.

day, Mary welcomes another's embodied humanity without ever using another person. She embodies chastity. *To welcome and yet remain whole and wholly oneself is the true call of chastity.* Chastity is the utter refusal to use any human in the name of pleasure, to subject your own pleasure to the greater reality of another whole image of God, like Jesus himself. Rather than being an individualistic practice of good behavior rewarded by pleasure, chastity is profoundly communal. Chaste people become sanctuaries in a violent world. They are safe. They become havens for the used and abused, for the little ones, for the brokenhearted. Chastity ends up being a form of justice and integrity—and love itself.

On Desire and Embodied Communion

The aching visibility of sexual desire combined with the heretical distrust of embodiment that I discussed in the last chapter often lead Christians to fixate on sex. We hide our vices and mistakes with crippling shame like Arthur Dimmesdale in *The Scarlet Letter,* or loudly denounce the sexual activities of others as the worst possible, repeatedly and publicly. One source of this shame is that many beloved children of God, medieval and modern alike, have been wrongly taught by Christians that they, as whole human beings, are worthless, lesser than, or outright ruined because of their sexual experiences and desires.[7]

---

7. Value-laden language is the trap of the so-called purity culture of the '90s and aughts that many of us grew up in. From comparisons to losing virginity like breaking things or pouring food coloring into water and noting it is no longer clear and perfect, to dehumanizing women's bodies by calling them "stumbling blocks," much damage has been done with this framing of sexual morality.

Let me be utterly clear to reject this feature of purity culture before I continue. One's sexual experiences and desires have *no relationship to one's worth as a human being.* God loves you. He does not love virgins more than sexually active people. He does not love straight people more than gay people. He does not love married people more than single people. "Come and see," Christ beckons (John 1:39). *I loved you long before you loved me,* he says (1 John 4:19). He loves. He is Love. His love as his divine character is radically independent of the circumstances of your life. Each one of us is ever held in that unchanging love.

The second thing we must hold in tension as we explore these words is that lust is not the same as sexual desire. Chastity is one of the daughters of temperance, the great cardinal virtue of "selfless self-love." Temperance helps us to regulate and enjoy bodily pleasures without trampling over those around us and hurting our own selves in that process. Chastity belongs to the same category as sobriety or abstinence. Like hunger and thirst, sexual desire is a natural desire. We embodied creatures are yearners at heart, made for desire in many ways: food, drink, fellowship, love, beauty, and most of all, God. Sexual desire neither fulfills our humanity nor undermines it. The significant difference is that one cannot die from not having sex as one would without eating or drinking. Sexual desire is one piece in the puzzle of our natural human longing for embodied communion.

Like hunger and thirst, we can experience pleasure through sexual desire, especially when that desire is sharpened, then satiated. This is not by itself a vicious habit. Yet like all pleasures, we can elevate it, desire it, shape our lives around it in a way that prevents full flourishing as created persons in community. We conflate pleasure with the embodied communion we crave. For we too easily let our pleasures rule our behavior, shape how we see the world, overcome our other desires, like loving others well in the beloved community of God. Such is the misshapen desire and practice we call lust.

Furniture in the Pleasure Tent

From demons lurking where amorous couples embrace, to a lascivious nun harvesting fleshy male members from a penis tree (I am not making this up), medieval artists represented lust with gleeful creativity.[8] But perhaps the most insightful portrayal of lust comes from the infamous Hieronymus Bosch. Bosch's paintings of hell have inspired modern art in their creepy-crawly, torturous depiction of demons and sinners. You'd expect that he would portray lust in one of these more outlandish ways too. But no—on his *Table of the Seven Deadly Sins* now at the Prado in Madrid, "Luxuria" is relatively tame.[9] In a pastel pink tent, two couples lounge about, casually embracing, watching two clowns cavort before them. Various musical instruments lie scattered on the grass in front of the tent. Off to the side, refreshments sit on a table. One of the clowns hits the other in the rear with a wooden spoon. The whole scene baffles rather than arouses.

---

8. See, respectively, detail of temptation by lechery, from Matfre Ermengaud, *Breviari d'Amor,* London, British Library, first quarter of the fourteenth century, Royal MS 19 C 1, f. 33r; a bas-de-page from a fourteenth-century *Roman de la Rose,* Paris, Bibliothèque nationale de France, MS. Fr. 25526, f. 106v.

9. Hieronymus Bosch, *Table of the Seven Deadly Sins,* ca. 1505–1510, Madrid, Museo del Prado.

Hieronymus Bosch, "Luxuria," detail from *Table of the Seven Deadly Sins*, oil on wood, ca. 1505–1510, Museo del Prado, Madrid.
Artefact / Alamy Stock Photo

Lust often flowers among other sensual delights. Take note of the music, the food, and the drink. But the clowns hint at more. In their capering, they tell us that all lust originates in folly. Such stupidity goes beyond the hero or heroine who repeatedly makes silly decisions in a romantic comedy. Pope Gregory the Great describes the origin of lust as "foolish looking" or "foolish listening."[10] The couples watching the clowning model the foolish beginnings of lust. We look at bodies and admire human beauty frequently. But when we *indulge* ourselves with such looking, we run into trouble. There is a habit of looking

10. *The Book of Vices and Virtues: A Fourteenth Century English Translation of the Somme Le Roi of Lorens d'Orleans*, ed. W. Nelson Francis (Oxford: Oxford University Press, 1998), 43.

informed by recklessness. Such intentional looking distinguishes the vice of lust from the eye happening to glance over an underwear ad or admiring the beauty of an attractive fellow human being. We hear Jesus himself telling his followers to take out their own eye if they lust (Matt. 5:29). Lust is in the eye (or ear) of the beholder, defying every make-believe myth of "the woman who asked for it."[11]

From foolish looking or listening, one moves into being ready to "delight privately" in these sights and sounds, according to Gregory.[12] It's the pleasure that is yours alone and foremost, secret, not to share. Such private delight strips bodies down into tools for present pleasure, whether that is the literal pleasure of the body or the powerful pleasure of being desired, in culturally acceptable and culturally unacceptable ways. The point is, however, that both foolish looking and private delight take place long before any touching, consensual or otherwise. They belong to a particular and habituated way of looking and moving through the world as an individual consumer, even when it comes to other embodied souls. *This is how* I *like it. This is what* I *want.* In private delight, relationships become burdensome: They are distractions and impediments to the potential pleasures at hand.

At last, lust can culminate—though, again, it does not have to—into the desired sexual act. We are beginning to recognize, more than our medieval forebears, how private delights can take dark turns into action. In lust I act as though you are not another

11. Eyes and a mind ready for private delight will take anything—a Victorian ankle's miraculous emergence from miles of skirt—for its solitary pleasures. The idiotic refrain "modest is hottest" reveals the paucity of how a lot of Christians treat modesty and the sick core of lust's private delights. Modesty, a real good, becomes short-circuited back into sexual gratification, a man's pleasure in a woman's dress, and immodesty an easy target for deflecting blame.

12. *Book,* 43.

whole human. This is what consent is theoretically supposed to fix in modern sexual ethics, but it cannot in full. Consent-based ethics offers only an ethical floor.[13] There is a user mentality even in socially licit lust. For the private delights of lust do not only appear in obviously terrible acts like assault or coercion; they pop up even in consensual sex, even in marriage itself. Flirting at the office with an attractive coworker to boost the old self-esteem. Porn or fantasizing that avoid the demands of attention and submission to a full, real human being in favor of erotic fantasy. Even fully consensual, desired casual sex is not capable of being a full act of embodied love. It remains primarily for one's private delights. It does not particularly matter who your partner is, as long as they are willing and attractive. The personal has gone.

Medieval writers even describe something curious that they called adultery within marriage: when one wants sex, and one's partner is merely a convenient accessory to that desire.[14] We see this today in many Christian expectations for marriage, in what might be called the "smokin' hot wife" rhetoric. Before marriage, no sex. After marriage, anything goes, and one partner (usually the wife) *owes* particular sexual acts to a spouse even if one is uncomfortable with it. This too is lust.[15] If a marriage exists only for self-gratification, whether sexual pleasure, a fantasy of domesticity and fairy-tale endings, or even only procreation, then it too cannot escape depersonalization. For though other human

---

13. See Christine Emba's *Rethinking Sex: A Provocation* (Sentinel, 2022) for an interview-based exploration of the modern sexual ethic of consent and its shortcomings.

14. For instance, *Fasciculus Morum*, 681.

15. I take this name from the rhetoric that still emerges from certain churches all the time, recently documented in Christianity Today's *The Rise and Fall of Mars Hill* podcast.

beings offer opportunities and space to practice virtues, no person can "fix" lust in another person.

Bosch's tepidly embracing men and women, supposedly the subjects of the scene, are ultimately inconsequential. In their insignificance, they look like more objects. Bosch knew that the foremost actions of lust do not occur while touching another person's body or your own body at all. *They have already taken place in the mind.* The pink pleasure tent is the room of the mind. In there, the nondescript men and women are pieces of furniture, even if respectfully treated, even if they get as much pleasure out of it as their partner. They function the same as the abandoned musical instruments on the ground or the forgotten tray of refreshments in the corner. You don't need to know anything about them, you don't need to care for them, they don't even need to be in the room with you—but they can still give you pleasure. Rather than meeting one another in our weakness and need in relationship in full personhood, we want the pleasures of sex and a mimicry of union without the work of close attention to another human being. It turns out that everyone is clowning.

A Tale of Two Chastities

Toward the end of the Middle Ages, a person named Rate transcribed a series of romances, saints' lives, religious lyrics, and advice poems into a volume now inelegantly named Codex Ashmole 61. (I get a kick out of Rate's habit of concluding these choices with *Amen quod Rate,* or, Amen says Rate.) Ashmole 61 is a book with what we would now anachronistically call middle-class values; religious devotion, business savvy, and pains to teach good manners all appear repeatedly.[16] In this smorgasbord, readers catch a glimpse of two chastities that offer us a challenge as we begin to understand this difficult virtue.

How the Good Wife Teaches Her Daughter

Early on, one encounters "How the Good Wife Taught Her Daughter," where a mother teaches her teenage daughter how to comport herself appropriately as she enters adulthood. The mother recommends the daughter to take the Eucharist regularly, walk to church even in the rain, bake bread for neighbors who need help, save money and use possessions well, and stay calm in arguments with your husband. And—chastity. The mother's recommendations for practicing chastity can be roughly summed up in this line: "Bide thou at home, my daughter dear."[17] The daughter is not to go places where men can become too familiar, like taverns and marketplaces. She is not to speak to men in public, just politely dismiss them. She should not even look at them, at least not for long. And when she has a daughter of her own, she should marry her off quickly: "For maidens, they be lonely / And thereby nothing is safe."[18] Nothing of this sort of highly gendered social and sexual behavior is found in the companion in Ashmole 61 to the Good Wife, "How the Wise Man Teaches His Son." These tidbits are common advice about practicing chastity for young women at the end of the Middle Ages. They are of a piece, but more practical for daily life, with what

16. The introduction by editor George Shuffelton helpfully lays out these themes in their contexts, *Codex Ashmole 61: A Compilation of Popular Middle English Verse* (Medieval Institute Publications, 2008).

17. "How the Good Wife Taught Her Daughter," L. 77, modern English translation mine in all Ashmole texts.

18. "Good Wife," ll. 181–4.

one penitential manual says with approval of the Virgin Mary's chastity: "It is said of the Blessed Virgin that, among the other aspects of her purity, she spoke so little that in the Gospel she is found to have spoken to only four persons, namely her son, the angel, Elizabeth, and John and the servants at the marriage."[19]

Women's silence is often connected to women's chastity. What a dull version of the Mary compared with the one we meet elsewhere, who in Marian apparitions speaks in the viewer's native tongue, whose vibrant yes offers home to God!

"The Good Wife" only gives us a list of rules, advice not all that dissimilar in spirit to the list of good and bad behavior I was taught as a teenager. We are often tempted, life-hack-like, to shrink chastity down into a list of prohibitions. As Christians, we believe some sexual prohibitions to be very good.[20] Marriage vows offer structure and safety to us tempested and imperfect human beings as we learn to love other whole human beings well. [21] I believe that, regarding sexual relationships, only in marriage do we know each other well enough to begin to avoid subordinating another whole person to our bodily pleasure.

But rules can never show us the deeper way. From Roman culture to the present day, such rule-based "chastity" has traditionally determined who is good enough to be Jesus's bride, or a bride in general, and who is impure, defiled, stained, left dangling on the outskirts of the kingdom like baggage.[22] Compare this with

19. *Fasciculus Morum*, 705.

20. Even the most liberal advocates for sexual liberation believe in condoms, spoken consent, and so on. No one believes sex without any boundaries is a good thing if they are being honest.

21. Much more could be said about the complexities and goods of the sacrament of marriage, but that is beyond the purview of this chapter.

22. Pieper notes how "the term defilement is almost never applied to other sins" outside of sexuality, *Cardinal Virtues*, 170.

the loving, listening, healing behavior of Christ in the Gospels as he meets women who have sinned sexually or dwell on the margins of society because of cultural bodily impurity (John 4; John 8:1–11; Mark 5:25–34). Paul warns us of shrinking Love down into the Law in too many places to list. One of my favorite modern-day theologians, Eugene Peterson, writes,

> If something is going to be done about sin, it is not going to be along the line of laws and rules, codes and regulations. . . . Sin is a violation of the essential personal nature of human life with one another and with God. We don't sin against a commandment; we sin against a person. Sin is not an offense against justice; sin is an offense against a living soul. Sin is not sexual impropriety; sin is the debasement of a man, a woman, a child. Sin is not a violation of the law of the land or the rules of a house; sin is a violation of a personal relationship.[23]

The essence of chastity is joyful and true relationship with the living God who dwells in your very body, relationship with other humans that witnesses to their full personhood, and an integration of our desire to love ourselves and love God in our present bodies, in our neighbors' present bodies. Such a foundation expands into real human yeses and nos regarding sexual conduct, but it can't be confined to them.

Saint Margaret of Antioch

Good thing our friend Rate is not done yet. Keep reading, and you meet one of the ubiquitous saints' lives of the day: a

---

23. Eugene Peterson, *Tell It Slant* (Eerdmans, 2008), 186–87.

Middle English Life of St. Margaret of Antioch.[24] Long associated with chastity, childbirth, and virginity, Margaret was one of the Fourteen "Holy Helpers" of the Middle Ages whose iconography appears in manuscript after manuscript, church after church. Another was Saint Catherine of Alexandria. She was a brilliant unmarried scholar who debated a multitude of pagan scholars and defeated them all, leading to her eventual martyrdom. These chaste saints were two of the three voices, along with the Archangel Michael, that Saint Joan of Arc would hear in Domrémy, France, in the fifteenth century. Joan would go on to lift the siege on Reims and crown Charles VII king of France before her own martyrdom.

That's quite the trio of women who undermine the feminine rule book that characterize the Good Wife's chastity. Clearly, there is power in their chastity, a welcome and fulfillment of need in community rather than a distortion of or turning away from it. In these women, we recognize the contours of a radical *embodied* wholeness and devotion to Jesus. In the medieval era, such countercultural behavior would be publicly celebrated only in virginity, which was a state more highly valued than marriage. But the stories of these women offer intriguing possibilities for why chastity should matter to us right now, men and women alike.

Margaret was a Christian raised by a pagan father, and at fifteen, "a fair woman, and bold" who tended her flock of sheep.[25] Her beauty attracted the attention of the passing pagan king, Olibrius. The king offers her all earthly pleasures, all fleshly joys, gold and riches all for her own if she agrees to marry him.

---

24. Saint Margaret's authenticity is in doubt—but that doesn't necessarily make her less of a teacher!

25. "St. Margaret," Codex Ashmole 61, l. 68.

Margaret refuses. At last Olibrius pleads with her to have mercy on "her fair flesh" or he will torture and imprison her. Her response:

> For thy gods in which you believe
> They are as dumb as any stone.
> My lord to me is full kind;
> He shall never leave my mind.
> Even if your hope concerns my flesh
> To do your will hard or tender,
> Or rend the flesh from the bone,
> Power over my soul you will get none.[26]

Olibrius may be able to torture her flesh, but he cannot touch her in her wholeness as beloved. Margaret models an important aspect of chastity: to recognize that the body, though good, is not the be-all and end-all. Out of this freedom, action flows. In this freedom, one can reject both using and being used.

After Margaret is thrown in prison, a demon comes to slay her in the guise of a dragon green as grass with bright fire burning in his jaws. Reasonably, she throws herself trembling on the ground and begins to pray. The dragon swallows her whole, body and bone. But it is not enough: Margaret bursts out of the dragon's belly. She stands upon the dragon carcass, "glad in heart and mild in mood."[27] Then, the dragon-demon's brother, Beelzebub himself, comes to scare and slay her. He proudly announces that he creates strife everywhere he goes so that people kill one another;

---

26. "St. Margaret," ll. 258–265.
27. "St. Margaret," l. 320.

he torments the beasts harrowing the fields to create food; he especially torments pregnant women and their babies. He is the enemy of the generation of life. Margaret beats him with a cross and ties the bedraggled demon up with her head covering. Yes, one of the items of clothing long associated with womanly purity!

When Olibrius checks on her, she invites him again to baptism. He, in what he thinks is a delicious irony, submerges her in boiling water. It does nothing to Margaret, who preaches the gospel from her cauldron as hundreds convert in the face of her witness. After a few more tries, she dies at last, assuring people in her death that she will intercede for them in eternity, especially pregnant women. *Amen, quod Grace.*

While the Good Wife seems more "realistic"—we are, after all, more likely to look too long at an attractive person than fend off marriage proposals from a pagan king—Margaret's chastity is more *real*. We begin to comprehend how what the Good Wife teaches as chastity is only a smallish form of continence, a self-control: often good but insubstantial, like a husband who stays begrudgingly faithful in his body to his wife, like a girl who stays home from the marketplace to show her purity. The desire is not behind it. Margaret shows us single-minded defiance against those who would reduce her to her body, and full-hearted desire for a soul-and-body existence as lover of Christ.

As Margaret defies social norms and disobeys all male authority figures in both the patriarchal society of Ashmole 61 and of her own fantastical time period, some of the more normative behavioral aspects are stripped away, and we better understand the habit of love called chastity. Margaret fully inhabits herself, her body. Even though her story has been heavily mythologized, she is a whole person. Neither gold nor pleasure nor even pain can lure her from her calling as Christ's beloved. Powerful and yet still on her way to death, she loves others, she looks to her community and advocates for them in the certainty of her belovedness. And as Christ's beloved, she neither uses other bodies nor consents to be used for the sake of the flesh's comfort. Margaret is free even while in chains. She is herself yet in relationship, chaste but not alone, embodied and transcendent all at once.

Fruits and Flowers

If you're not a virgin martyr, what does living a life of chastity look like, beyond not using others for pleasure? Plunge into medieval writing on chastity, and you enter a glorious garden of fragrant growth: sweet-scented cedar, lofty above the forest roof; aromatic, delicate roses, their oil used to bathe the limbs and torso and perfume the body; pomegranates, rosy red and gorgeous, cooling ardor and satiating hunger of the body on hot days; cinnamon, sweetening the breath, giving flavor and spice to food; grapes, ripe and hanging heavy on a vine, making joy in the form of heady wine; palm trees, medicinal, which stay green even in the dead of winter, bearing sweet and sticky dates.[28]

Such metaphors can be taken rather straightforwardly considering the fruit of many marriages: children. This is true, but it is incomplete. Our friend Margaret throws out the deeply misguided modern suggestion that chaste fruitfulness in life is tied exclusively to childbearing and marriage.[29] Fruitfulness is a universal promise

28. These images appear all over medieval writing on chastity, but this specific list comes from *Summa virtutum* on the chastity of Mary, 304–24.

29. Let us not forget that medieval people took Paul quite literally. Intentional virginity

of the life of chastity. I love the anecdote that the Roman Catholic bishop Erik Varden narrates in his recent book on chastity: "When I entered monastic life, an old monk said to me, 'Remember, you've no right to live a sterile life!' I have always been grateful for that remark. It qualifies celibacy and reveals its meaning. The celibate, no less than the married man or woman, is called to a generative life of communion, to see and to be seen, to love and to be loved."[30]

The sexual drive is a drive to life. When it is oriented toward wholeness, of oneself and of other humans, toward personal relationship, it gives birth, whether in the context of singleness or marriage. Unlike our modern-day associations of chastity with cold disembodiedness, chastity is fundamentally life-giving: aromatic, blooming, fruitful, heady. To what does chastity give birth?

Chastity gives birth to justice. In justice, we honor other people's full humanity. When we see one another in full, and not as potential vehicles for our pleasure, nor threats to it or ourselves, we can render to one another what we owe in love, in imitation of the justice of Jesus Christ.

Chastity gives birth to hospitality and welcome. Other beloved ones of God are safe with us when we do not wish to consume them, to possess their bodies and depersonalize them, or even to love someone and then leave them when it no longer suits us. In practicing chastity, we protect one another, like Saint Margaret interceding for pregnant mothers and women everywhere. We become refuges for the little ones of Jesus in a violent, using world.

Chastity gives birth to the ability to see beauty wherever it is. Thomas Aquinas recognizes temperance's special relationship to

---

was always morally superior to marriage, as was celibate widowhood (see, for instance, Aquinas, *ST* II-II.152).

30. Erik Varden, *Chastity: Reconciliation of the Senses* (Bloomsbury, 2023), 107.

beauty.[31] When we are in beautiful places or with beautiful people, we often want them for ourselves—to live there, to own that, to be with them, to be like them. We reduce our pleasure to whether it belongs to us, whether we can possess this attractive place, person, or thing. Practicing temperance helps us learn how to take joy in the things and people that do not belong to us or do not directly benefit us. Varden comments, "To do something beautiful for its own sake, for the intrinsic delight of it, without thought of gain: this, I'd say, is a way of beginning to live chastely in this world."[32] In chastity, we are freed into admiring the beauty that exists as it is, in our spouse, children, home, neighbor, art. We are also freed into creating beauty that is just beautiful for its own sake, loved for its sheer existence.

At last, chastity gives birth to true relationship, intimacy, and self-giving in community. We humans were made to give ourselves, to receive one another in joy and gratitude, to know and be known in our fullness as unique persons yet each an image of divinity. In true self-giving, whether in singleness or marriage, we become the Eucharistic body of Christ, set apart, broken, given, received as we are. In this self-giving, we also imitate the communion of the triune God, in which each Person constantly pours out in love and joy into the other and into creation itself, being one, though yet three. Real knowledge of others and oneself, real intimacy, is possible only within relationship, which presupposes and requires vulnerability, trust, love. Depersonalization and use destroy one's ability to receive each full and unique gift of each child of God as they are.

---

31. Aquinas, *ST* II-II.141.2.ad3. Insensibility to beauty is especially related to both gluttony and lust (Aquinas, *ST* II-II.142.1). See also Pieper, *Cardinal Virtues*, 167; Wirzba, *Food & Faith: A Theology of Eating* (Cambridge University Press, 2011), 10–11; Saint Catherine of Siena, *Dialogue*, on looking with God's eyes on the beauty and dignity of the human creature, number 1.

32. Varden, *Chastity*, 59.

Chastity as Contemplation

We are created as embodied souls and called to fully embrace the life of the body with love. We are also to recognize that there is more, so much more, beyond the limits of our skin, nerves, stomach, sex organs. If I can't recognize my own limitations, the good Grace Hamman–shaped being moving through the universe by touch and instinct and taste and thought, and the good outside myself, whether that's nature or another human, which lives beyond my mind and nerve endings and stomach, then I will always seek to possess, own, explain, benefit, whether in body or in mind. And sometimes I will call that love. But I will not be submitting to the reality of the other creature outside what I can immediately understand. I will be forcing that person or gift into my space, my understanding, my pleasures, like a square peg into a round hole.

God, instead of doing that to us—and in our mess, we would quite deserve it—comes to us, is like us, in full communion, submits to love and limitation and dies on a cross. In his very body he raises us out of our mess into glory. Our love and knowledge of one another is invitational, relational, requiring mutual submission, attention, joy in another's full being. In the appreciation of your wholeness, I become more whole.

True chastity becomes a practice of contemplation. Where is the beauty and pleasure that I can see and love for itself? Can I start to let go of the desire to possess things for myself, or even to see only their usefulness to me? Have I submitted to the reality of the other person, and of myself, of God? Will you consent to a union that you cannot own, that always goes beyond you into reality itself and yet happens in your very body?

This is the question of annunciation.

Practices and Prayer

To no man owe anything, but love together. For he that loveth his neighbor hath fulfilled the law. For thou shalt do no lechery, thou shalt not steal, thou shalt not say false witnessing, thou shalt not covet the thing of thy neighbor, and if there be any other commandment, it is in-stored in this word, thou shalt love thy neighbor as thyself. The love of neighbor worketh no evil, therefore love is the fulfilling of the law. And we know this time, that the hour is now that we rise from sleep; for now our health is nearer than when we first believed. The night went before, but the day hath neared. Therefore cast we away the works of darknesses, and be we clothed in the armors of light. In the day we wander honestly, not in superfluous feasts and drunkenness, not in beds and unchastities, not in strife and envy; but be ye clothed in the Lord Jesus Christ, and do ye not the busyness of flesh in desires. (Rom. 13:8–14, Middle English Bible, my updated spelling)

Practices

- Reflect on this question and honestly share with a trusted friend, family member, or spouse: How do I attempt to possess or control or use other people?
- Go out of your way to look at beauty this week, in nature, in books, in art. Receive it as it is. This is good practice for receiving other people in their wholeness.
- If you have been struggling with lust, try fasting in community, the ancient recommendation for dealing with bodily temptation. Invite someone to join you in the

practice. The traditional day for fasting is Friday, but you can freely adapt.

- Read further about chastity: *Chastity* by Erik Varden, *The Flowing Light of the Godhead* by Mechthild of Magdeburg, *Laurus* by Eugene Vodolazkin.

Prayer

Lord Jesus, make me chaste in my body and soul. Forgive me for the ways in which I have reduced or used my neighbor or my body for my own pleasure. Thank you for giving me my good body and all its pleasures and for creating the beauty of humanity. Give me the strength and humility to resist using other people for my own pleasures, in big and little ways. I thank you and your mother for modeling a life lived wholly in relationship. Fill me up with that kind of love and the welcome, justice, and safety that it brings to others around me. Let me recognize and embrace the beauty of the world. Amen.

CONCLUSION

FURTHER DOWN THE OLD PATHS

Roads go ever ever on
Under cloud and under star,
Yet feet that wandering have gone
Turn at last to home afar.
Eyes that fire and sword have seen
And horror in the halls of stone
Look at last on meadows green
And trees and hills they long have known.

—J. R. R. Tolkien

This book is begun by God's gift and his grace,
but it is not yet finished, as to my sight.

—Julian of Norwich

This book was not written impartially. I did not want these virtue and vice words to be flimsy cardboard words of obligation anymore. I wanted to give the tiger back her teeth, to re-fang something a little wild and beautiful. I wanted to think with them from my modern-day perspective; I *want to love them,* like Julian and Thomas and Francis and Catherine did (and do). In that desire to love, I have tried to untangle these words from the shame and confusion that obscure their relationship to the life of love.

For the virtues are only and ever about love, in the end. Not a love offered in soapy sentimentality nor love deployed in a convenient catchphrase but a love that is becoming enfleshed in you and me, that takes form and life in our own bodies. These ancient words remain only abstract concepts until you and I fill them up with love. Every virtue is just love in disguise. Each one is another facet of love's unfolding creativity in acknowledging the reality of God, yourself, another human, or creation. Humility, patience, meekness, fortitude, constancy, mercy, abstinence, chastity—all variations on the same theme, like Bach played a hundred different ways by a hundred different performers on their hundred different instruments.

How shall we now live? At times while writing, I have become overwhelmed with the beauty of the virtues, but even more so, their challenge. How can I practice these virtues in my own time and place, burdened with my particular burdens and weak with my particular weaknesses? What if I am not capable? What if I am just not as good as this person or that? This virtue feels impossible, that one far away. My questions reveal an attitude that many of us take for granted: that the virtues are individual achievements that I can plug back into my worth, into *my* holiness. I constantly fall back into the mentality of *achieving* the virtues, similar to my mindset the year I took the SATs. The whole and holy life is not a Scantron sheet with right and wrong bubbles to shade with my No. 2 pencil or click on a screen. It does not come with a convenient score meant to help me compare myself to and understand my personal superiority over—or inferiority to—other high school kids.

Sadly, also kind of hilariously, this desire to perform leads me right back into the original sin of all sins: pride. In pride, I constantly look at my superiority as proof of my worth, shielding myself against my inevitable failures. I fear flunking the virtues. I have to laugh at myself, for in my fears of personal failure I fall into pride all over again. "The root of all sin is fear," writes the great modern-day theologian Herbert McCabe,

> the very deep fear that we are nothing; the compulsion, therefore, to make something of ourselves, to construct a self-flattering image of ourselves that we can worship, to believe in ourselves—our fantasy selves. I think all sins are failures in being realistic; even the simple everyday sins of the flesh, that seem to move from mere childish greed for pleasure, have their deepest origin in anxiety about whether we really matter, the anxiety that makes us desperate for self-reassurance.[1]

The whole and holy life requires a reorientation in desire that flows outward into my patterns of thought and habits in the world. There is no more need to prove *my* worth. There is no more measurement of how good of a job *I'm* doing. There are, of course, failures and victories over my fears and selfishness, which are other kinds of tests to pass, but these no more reflect my belovedness to God than a scab on my knee.

The virtuous life is not like a test in which I prove my worthiness and get a good grade. I leave you with three counterimages, some of them a reminder of what we have already explored, to kill the temptation to understand the virtuous life as a measuring stick. What is this life like?

The Virtuous Life Is like a Pilgrimage

You are a pilgrim on your way somewhere. You might be like Chaucer's clueless Prioress or saucy Wife or noble Knight or

1. Herbert McCabe, *God, Christ, and Us*, ed. Brian Davies (London: Continuum, 2003), 17–18.

obscene Miller. You might take wrong turns, or you might get waylaid at a dirty inn for some time. You might even be shipwrecked. But you are going somewhere. You are on the road with particular companions, on your way to a kingdom that has come and not yet come. The virtues always have an end, a goal, a *telos*. This end is life together with Jesus in the kingdom of heaven.

I often think about how to live together in peace and joy in this coming kingdom, all the little brokennesses will have to be fixed. Not patched up, like a shoddy Scotch-tape job, or covered up, like the bitter pain that one has simply learned to hide well around certain people, but fully healed. For such healing to happen, we will face all the things we have done and left undone. Everyone will. Who knows what forms this reconciliation will take? Regardless of that form, it will bring us more healing, less time wandering lost and darkened ways in the night, or spent in dirty inns away from home, if we walk toward wholeness now.

This feels daunting, but it is true for all journeys. To start a long journey, we open a door; we step outside the familiar confines. Even if we do not exactly know how to get to where we want to be, we know we must take those first steps. Henri Nouwen wrote that in the spiritual life, "you already know the little steps, even if you don't know the big ones." He goes on,

> You don't need to know the big steps to take the little steps. You only have to take one step at a time. The interesting thing is that the person who is in touch with the Lord knows what those little steps are. For example, we could say, "I am not going to speak about that person that way anymore. I am not going to gossip." It is a little thing. No one notices. We still don't like that person, but at least we are not going to say bad things about them anymore.

> Little step. The next step might be that we smile at them. Then we invite them over. Before we know it we are friends. If we look back we see it was a long journey of little steps.[2]

Only through small steps do we reach any destination at all. Before you know it, you are halfway there. And these strides only come from the small faithful actions of refusing to give up, of moving your feet onward. Real home awaits.

The Virtuous Life Is like a Garden

Balance the active steps of the road with the garden, which reminds us that all we receive, all that grows, is a gift. One medieval author writes of how holy Scripture "likens a person's soul to a fair garden full of green trees and good fruit."[3] The writer uses the Song of Songs to imagine the soul as an enclosed garden, protected by angels and the grace of God. "This garden is planted by the great Gardener, by God the Father, who softens the hard ground of the heart. He makes it treatable as wax well-tempered to take the print of the seal, as good black earth, well-arrayed, waiting for the good grafts for which it is worthy. These grafts are the good virtues that the Holy Ghost bedews with generous grace."[4]

We weed, we cut judiciously, we harvest in season—the small steps—but the seeds themselves are miraculous. The joy of growth

---

2. Henri Nouwen, *Following Jesus: Finding Our Way Home in an Age of Anxiety* (Convergent Books, 2019), 43.

3. Royal 18, *Two Middle English Translations of Friar Laurent's Somme le Roi: Critical Edition*, ed. Emmanuelle Roux (Turnhout, Belgium: Brepols, 2010), 61.

4. Royal 18, *Two Middle English Translations*, 61.

is miraculous. The earth, the water—all are gifts. The Lord has already deemed the ground of our hearts worthy. We are invited into participating in our own sanctification (Phil. 2:12–13).

And each garden is gloriously different. The medieval writer was thinking of the kind of enclosed gardens filled with fruit trees that were tended with love at the great houses and monasteries of the Middle Ages. But I was meditating on this passage as I recently hiked Mount Elbert, the tallest mountain in the Rockies. One of the most miraculous things about being up there, so far above where trees can survive, is that other things are alive in these harsh conditions. No great oak or fruitful apple tree or even a tomato plant could thrive up there. But the tiniest of wildflowers beam along the path, bees buzz among them, and the marvelously shaggy Rocky Mountain goats laze in the sun or graze in peace. It is a garden of its own, unlike any I could have ever foreseen until I saw it myself.

So too each soul-garden has different seeds, different climates, different fruits. I may not resemble Saint Catherine of Siena or Harriet Tubman or Dietrich Bonhoeffer. My soul is called to flower forth and fruit in its particularity nonetheless. The virtues are so beautiful, partially because the saints who live them share nothing in common but the greatness of their love. This is the creativity of the virtues, of learning the habits of not using one another, of seeing one another, of knowing one another and ourselves, of loving God with whole heart, mind, and body.

In the virtues, we do not pound ourselves into the identical shape of something or someone else, like dough by cookie cutter, or brick and mortar and stucco into the same shape of houses on the suburban street. People are not sugar cookies nor, praise God, the split-levels that plague my Denver suburb. It is the vices that conform us into the same dreary old obsessions, insecurities, and self-absorption. There is a radical diversity within the life of love, a universal and graced calling into holiness responsive to every person's own context, time, gifts, and burdens. We are to conform only to Jesus Christ, he who is endless, everlasting, beautiful beyond reckoning, who has chosen us, in all our difference and strangeness, to be his body on earth.

The Virtuous Life Is like a Story

Stories have beginnings, middles, and ends. There are times in the story when it seems so dark that nothing can ever change. There seems to be no possibility of hope or redemption. How shall I live then?

The moral philosopher Alasdair MacIntyre wrote that one cannot answer the question of what one ought to do unless "I first answer the question of what story or stories do I find myself a part?"[5] He is speaking largely of the human traditions to which we belong as members of various communities. But you and I also belong to a much bigger story that envelops all these smaller stories and contexts. We are already part of something eternal that is not dependent on one's individual goodness nor hampered permanently by error or evil. You and I have belonged to Jesus since the foundation of the world. That will be the beginning and the end of every story we tell. Out of this story flows everything else: all beauty, all dying to the silliest fantasies of sufficiency and self-importance, all

5. Alasdair MacIntyre, *After Virtue: A Study in Moral Theory*, 3rd ed. (Notre Dame: University of Notre Dame Press, 2008), 216.

joys, all loves, and all life. The story started before you; it will go on after you, and with you, into the unending kingdom. When we feel daunted or even defeated by the call of sanctification, we remember that we are in the story that has not ended yet.

How are *you* specifically invited into love, whole person? You who raises children in Denver, who creates beautiful things in Bloomington, who pastors in Durham, who studies in New York, who teaches in Guadalajara, who counsels adolescents in Tempe, who feeds stroke victims in Asheville, who films documentaries in Portland, who tends language in Grand Rapids? No human language can ultimately describe the beauty of what you are becoming in the wholeness of divine love.

I leave you to your learning and living, with a medieval promise that ends a far older book of virtues and vices. It is a testament to the glory that grows along the path you wander into wholeness, until at last all is illuminated:

> It passes all words, for heart nor strength nor thought nor tongue can tell what joy nor how deep is that peace that God has ordained for his friends; and therefore we jangle and speak insufficiently; wherefore we will say no more at this time, but here we leave our matter to the joy and bliss of our Lord, to whom be all thanks and worship, and that he may lead us into his fellowship, where there is life without end. So might it be—
> A . . . . . M . . . . . E . . . . . N[6]

6. *The Book of Vices and Virtues: A Fourteenth Century English Translation of the Somme Le Roi of Lorens d'Orleans*, ed. W. Nelson Francis (Oxford: Oxford University Press, 1998), 290.